The Letter of James

The Letter of James

A PASTORAL COMMENTARY

Addison Hodges Hart

CASCADE *Books* · Eugene, Oregon

THE LETTER OF JAMES
A Pastoral Commentary

Cascade Books
An Imprint of Wipf and Stock Publishers
199 W. 8th Ave., Suite 3
Eugene, OR 97401

www.wipfandstock.com

PAPERBACK ISBN: 978-1-5326-5014-7
HARDCOVER ISBN: 978-1-5326-5015-4
EBOOK ISBN: 978-1-5326-5016-1

Cataloguing-in-Publication data:

Names: Hart, Addison Hodges, author.

Title: The letter of James : a pastoral commentary / Addison Hodges Hart.

Description: Eugene, OR: Cascade Books, 2018 | Includes bibliographical references.

Identifiers: ISBN 978-1-5326-5014-7 (paperback) | ISBN 978-1-5326-5015-4 (hardcover) | ISBN 978-1-5326-5016-1 (ebook)

Subjects: LCSH: Bible. James—Commentary.

Classification: BS2785.53 .H365 2018 (print) | BS2785.53 2018 (ebook)

Manufactured in the U.S.A.   OCTOBER 3, 2018

*Dedicated with great affection to my son Addison
and to my daughter Anna.
Each of you has given me great joy in life, and my wish for you both is
abundance of peace, serenity, happiness, familial love, and full lives.*

"Do not explain your philosophy. Embody it."

- EPICTETUS

"To understand is easy; to practice is hard."

- BANKEI

CONTENTS

Introduction 1

  I. *Preliminaries* 3

  II. *Who was James "the Just" of Jerusalem?* 8

  III. *James: the "brother" of Jesus?* 15

  IV. *Was the Letter of James written by James or by someone else?* 18

  V. *The Spirit of this commentary* 22

  VI. *Outline of the Letter of James* 29

A Note About the Translation Used in this Book 31

Commentary 33
Concluding Comments 117

Introduction

This is a pastoral commentary. By that I mean that its primary focus is on the practical concerns of people seeking to live according to the gospel that Jesus proclaimed. I do not consider myself a theologian or scholar in the academic sense. For years, however, my vocation was that of a priest, pastor, and college chaplain, and this commentary on the Letter of James reflects my training and experience in those capacities. It is not addressed to the scholarly community, although I rely on what I have gleaned from it. It is primarily addressed to those—lay and ordained—who are actively engaged in building vital Christian communities.

James's letter is itself a thoroughly pastoral letter. Like the teachings of Jesus in the Synoptic Gospels, it is short on theory and long on pragmatics. It virtually eschews the merely conceptual and abstract ("You have faith that God is one? You are doing well. Even the daemonic beings have that faith, and they tremble"; Jas 2:19). It is concerned with religion, as we shall see below, and religion for James refers to how we live our lives.

James is a moralist in the best sense of that word. He is not given to "moralism"—to mere nagging or scolding—although he does excoriate those whom he believes deserve it. The rich, those who judge others, those who abuse others with their tongues—these, for example, come in for very strong words. But he is a moralist in the strict sense that he defends the morals that Jesus taught. His letter is, in spirit, a moral corrective. We forget sometimes that Jesus, as he is presented in the first three Gospels, did not preach mainly about himself, but about "the kingdom of God." By that phrase he meant a distinctive way of life, one that intentionally cuts against the grain of the world's (and the individual's) greed, power, lust, and exploitation of others. Jesus, then, was a moralist and James follows in his footsteps.

1

So this is a pastoral commentary on a pastoral epistle. My intention is to apply this letter to our contemporary communities, by first keeping a close eye on what James was saying to his own contemporaries. I will state here at the outset that the New Testament is not a monolithic "book" with a single portrait of Jesus and a single systematic theology. Like the Old Testament, it is a collection that presents us with differing voices and a variety of perspectives surrounding a central faith. None of the individual writers/editors whose work is included within it were writing "New Testament theology," but were instead addressing disciples who came from a variety of places and backgrounds and that faced various problems from without and within their communities. So it is that, say, the Gospel of John differs in its understanding of Jesus' person and message from Matthew's. The book of Revelation presents a picture of a warrior Jesus who looks quite different than the Jesus in Luke who prays that his Father forgive his executioners. Paul's Christology differs from Mark's. And so on. That the New Testament coheres for us is, in great part, because we have been taught in our ecclesiastical contexts to see it that way.

As we shall discuss below, the Letter of James stands out as a counter in some ways to a "gospel *about* Jesus" because—paradoxically, perhaps—it is so faithful to the gospel *of* Jesus. Paul and the Johannine writings, we must admit, are examples of the former. Jesus *becomes* for both "the gospel," as it were. For James, however, "the gospel" is not *about* Jesus—rather, it is about the "religion," *the way of life*, which Jesus taught us to live concretely.

With that provocative thought in mind, then, I propose to explore the background of this letter more deeply and the man who wrote it.

I.

Preliminaries

Martin Luther's assessment of the Letter of James as "an epistle of straw" is, of course, almost a cliché. But, having mentioned it here, it's also right to note that he withdrew the remark later. By "straw" he meant that the letter was useful for very little, if anything really. It was of a weak quality and not fit for building anything of lasting worth. This harsh assessment appeared only once, in the original version of Luther's *Preface to the New Testament* (1522), as part of a paragraph that also made judgments about other New Testament books. Thinking better of it later, Luther struck the comment, along with the entire paragraph in which it appeared, from the text in subsequent editions of his Bible.

The reformer's chief difficulty with James, which (despite his editing out the remark) he never abandoned, was that James did not express what he considered to be the most essential message *about* Christ. For Luther what was lacking was the good news itself. He asserted, and he went on asserting throughout his lifetime, that the Letter of James and the letters of Paul could not be reconciled. He did concede (surely backhanded praise, given Luther's views) that James was "a good book" because it set forth the *law* of God. By saying that it was an epistle of *law*, however, he was unmistakably implying that it was not a proclamation of the gospel—which, for Luther, was summed up in the phrase "justification by faith alone." There was irony in this, for—as Luther could not help but be uncomfortably aware—the *only* instance in the entire New Testament where the phrase "justified . . . by faith alone" appears is, in fact, in the Letter of James: "You see that a man is *justified by works and not by faith alone*" (Jas 2:24, RSV;

emphasis mine). And that was not what Luther wanted to hear, and hence his difficulty with "strawy" James.

But, even long before the age of Luther, the Epistle of James had been open to criticism for its supposed shortcomings. In the West, its authorship was held in some suspicion well into the fourth century; and, indeed, its genuineness was still in question as late as the sixteenth century, most notably by Luther's scholarly contemporaries, Erasmus and Cardinal Cajetan. In the Eastern churches, on the other hand, James had been included among the canonical books from early on, although Eusebius, writing in the 320s, ranked it among the "disputed" books (along with Jude, 2 Peter, and 2 and 3 John; see his *History of the Church*, III, 25). "Admittedly its authenticity is doubted," wrote Eusebius, "since few early writers refer to it" (*HC*, III, 26). Nevertheless, as Eusebius admitted, there had at least been a "few early writers" who referred to it. For example, *The Shepherd of Hermas*, a popular late first-century or early second-century Roman apocalyptic work, cited the Letter of James more often than it did any other epistle found in the New Testament canon. And indeed, by the end of the fourth century, James's place within the canon of the universal church was effectively and finally settled, its authority was deemed apostolic, and its author was generally accepted as being none other than James "the Just," the brother of the Lord, the first "bishop" of Jerusalem, one of the three whom Paul had referred to as the reputed pillars of the church (along with Peter and John; cf. Gal 1:9), and the adjudicator in the troublesome matter of how to accommodate uncircumcised gentile converts within the community of this new Jesus-centered variant of the Jewish religion (cf. Acts 15).

Although the question of its authenticity was one reason given for some to feel hesitant about it, there were possibly other concerns in the church about its validity. We have already noted its seemingly direct rebuttal of Paul's message, a subject we will come back to at some length in this commentary. Conspicuously, there was a certain *lack* of content in the letter that could well have seemed disturbing to some in these early Christian centuries. For instance, the letter mentions the name of Jesus only twice (1:1; 2:1). Likewise, Jesus' death and resurrection, so pivotal in other writings that were deemed canonical, are not a central theme in the book. Doctrinal orthodoxy, in fact, gives way to orthopraxy (right behavior and action) as the focus of James's concerns. Hesitancy about the Letter of James may have stemmed from a notable *absence* in it of specific doctrinal expectations.

When the New Testament canon was still in its formation, during the third and fourth centuries, the determinative criteria for including a book or epistle was to be found in the church's common *regula fidei*—the "rule of faith" or the creedal formula affirmed by the "orthodox" churches (one version of which is the Western church's "Apostles' Creed"). Right belief was the guiding feature in discerning which books should be received as inspired, apostolic, and universally authoritative. Such careful attentiveness to basic doctrine was directly in reaction to versions of the faith that had, over time, been deemed heterodox—and, in fact, some of the very communities that were seen to hold heterodox opinions also were known to revere the memory of the authority of James the Just. Worse, some of these communities explicitly, even bitterly, rejected the authority of the Apostle Paul, whose reputation in the "great church" had become unassailable. In other words, in those metropolitan churches (primarily Rome, but also Antioch and Alexandria), in which Paul, along with Peter, after their deaths, had come to occupy the central place as the revered apostles *par excellence*, it was supposed that what was professed should be absolutely true to the faith these two apostles (and their episcopal successors) were believed to have imparted. Thus, what was confessed *about* the Trinity and *about* the person and work of Christ had to be sound and untainted by heterodox notions. This conviction became even more pronounced when Christianity became at first *a* faith and eventually *the* faith of the Roman Empire, since it was the grand design of the emperors, beginning with Constantine, to have a united imperial church with a coherent and obligatory creed, under the supervision of orthodox bishops, planted firmly at the center of an orderly and pious realm. The Letter of James, lacking a clearly articulated orthodoxy, offered little of use for cementing such a strong confessional faith in the "one, holy, catholic, and apostolic church" of the Empire; and its implicit tension with the teaching of Paul, as found particularly in the latter's Epistles to the Romans and the Galatians, certainly might have been provocative.

There had been, as well, a lessening of the importance of the role Jesus' family had played in the early church, since the decades when its center was still in Jerusalem. They, and James in particular, had been acknowledged as the key figures in that first community of Jesus' followers. However, following the fall of Jerusalem in 71 AD, their influence was largely eclipsed outside Jewish Christian circles. The inevitable "gravitational" shift of ecclesiastical authority and influence, after the loss of the "mother church," to

5

newer centers in Antioch, Alexandria, and ultimately Rome, meant that James and the family of Jesus in Jerusalem were no longer at the heart of Christian identity. Peter, Paul, and Rome became that new center. The Letter of James, seen from this perspective, might be a surviving relic of a time when James still occupied a place as "first among equals" (as he did for a time), and thus able to pen what looks very much to be an "encyclical" letter, one intended for all the scattered communities of Christians. As mentioned above, the uncomfortable fact is that by the fourth century the remnant of the old Jewish Christian church, which had revered James for centuries, was held in suspicion for entertaining ideas deemed heretical by the now dominant imperial Roman church.

All this is inference, of course, but the fact remains that James's letter was a "disputed book"; and yet, regardless of that, it survived to make the canonical "final cut." One plausible reason for its final acceptance, one which I certainly have no difficulty accepting and do accept in this commentary, may simply have been that there was no good excuse not to believe it truly had come from the hand of James—that it was, in all probability, an authentic work that came with credentials too credible to be rejected out of hand, whatever its perceived deficiencies.

One aspect of the letter that could not be disputed was that, whereas it said little *about* Jesus, it undoubtedly reflected a familiarity with the authentic teachings *of* Jesus. Such texts as James 1:6 and 2:8, for example, have direct and obvious parallels to Jesus' own words (and, of course, we will deal with those texts in their proper places below). James's epistle can at times seem to be a restatement of the Sermon on the Mount (for example, compare Matt 5:9 with Jas 2:5; Matt 5:7 and 6:14 with Jas 2:13; Matt 5:11–12 with Jas 5:10; Matt 5:19 with Jas 2:10; Matt 5:34–37 with Jas 5:12; Matt 6:19 with Jas 5:2; Matt 6:34 with Jas 4:13–14; and Matt 7:24 with Jas 1:22–25). What we find in the letter, then, is not so much a religion about the person of Christ as a reiteration of the religion of Christ himself—what Jesus himself believed and taught his disciples about living in communion with God.

James is thoroughly pragmatic in his outlook as well as thoroughly immersed in the teachings of Jesus, his "brother" (a term we will look at more closely below). His exhortations are about living and doing, and the letter regards conceptual, confessional belief as something essentially lifeless unless it is energized by the "breath" or "spirit" of a lived, practical discipleship ("For just as the body without spirit [or, breath] is dead, so also faith without works is dead"; Jas 2:26). Because of its intimate familiarity with the core of Jesus' instruction to his followers, readers can feel them-selves near to Jesus, particularly as he is presented in the Gospel of Mat-thew, when one reads James. James retains many of the same emphases and inhabits the same thought-world as his Lord and brother.

This is, I suggest, an implicit argument in favor of James of Jerusalem as author of the epistle, rather than it being the work of someone writing in his name. It may, in fact, be one of the earliest of the New Testament books. There is nothing within the book to assign it decisively to a first-century date later than the death of James in 62. Attempts to date it later and assign it to a pseudonymous author have never risen above the speculative. To be sure, no one can assert conclusively that the letter is by James, but, by the same token, no one can assert conclusively that it is not. In this commen-tary, then, I adopt the judgment that it is James's own work.

II.

Who was James "the Just" of Jerusalem?

The earliest record in the New Testament that we have regarding James is found in the letters of Paul. He is not, of course, the only James in the New Testament. "James" or "Jacob" was a common name for Jews to bear, being the name of the Old Testament patriarch whose other, divinely bestowed name was "Israel." Named in the New Testament are also James, the son of Zebedee (Mark 1:19–20; 3:17), James, the son of Alphaeus (Mark 3:18; Acts 1:13), and James, the father of Judas (Luke 6:18). But it is doubtful that the name of the author of the epistle was meant to signify someone other than James of Jerusalem, "the brother of the Lord." It is Paul, whose authentic letters are considered to be the earliest writings in the New Testament, who provides us with some important details concerning James.

Paul informs us that James had been visited with an appearance of the risen Christ (1 Cor 15:7), and that he was one of the "pillars" of the church in Jerusalem (Gal 2:9), the one with whom Paul had consulted personally in that city (Gal 1:19), and whose influence, through his representatives, was felt as far as Antioch in Syria (Gal 2:12). We are given to understand that there was, at least at one point in their interactions, some tension between Paul and James (and, of course, with Peter, as well) over relations at table fellowship in Antioch between Jewish and gentile believers (cf. Gal 2:6, 11). Paul also leads us to believe that James probably was a married man (1 Cor 9:5).

Turning from Paul to the Gospels, all of which were written after Paul's death, we find that they tell how Jesus' family members not only were not initially followers of his message, but that they even worried for his sanity soon after he began his ministry. Mark 3:21 describes them as anxiously seeking for him in order to take him home, believing that "he was beside himself." In Mark 6, when Jesus passes through Nazareth, we are informed, through the mouths of those hearing him speak in the synagogue, that he had four brothers and more than one sister: "Is not this man the craftsman, the son of Mary and brother of James and Joses and Judas and Simon? And are not his sisters here with us?" (Mark 6:3).[1] The Gospel of John clearly concurs that Jesus' brothers were not among his early followers: "his brothers," the Evangelist writes flatly, "did not have faith in him." They are depicted as taunting him, in rough brotherly fashion perhaps, to go and show himself off "to the cosmos" (by doing so before the multitudes in Jerusalem) if he *really* was doing all the astounding things he was touted as having performed (John 7:3–5). At this early stage, James, along with Jesus' other brothers, shows no understanding of what Jesus is doing and proclaiming. We can suppose there is in this a true historical memory, given how greatly James and the family of Christ were later esteemed.

Lest we come too hastily to the conclusion that, perhaps, James was not regarded as a righteous man during the time that he and his brothers were dubious about Jesus' ministry, there is an intriguing fragment from a lost Gospel that provides us with an early tradition that he and the family had, in fact, been receptive of the message of John the Baptist before Jesus began his own ministry. The so-called *Gospel of the Nazarenes*, originally composed in Aramaic sometime before 200, tells how "the mother of the Lord and his brethren" urged Jesus to go with them to be baptized by John the Baptist for "the remission of sins."[2] If not a total fabrication, it may be seen as agreeing somewhat with the witness of Hegesippus (a second-century Jewish Christian, it should be noted, about whom more below), who wrote of James that he "was holy from his birth" and that he was someone "whom everyone from the Lord's time till our own has called the

---

1. Later traditions name the two sisters. The apocryphal fourth/fifth-century *History of Joseph the Carpenter* calls them Assia and Lydia, while the fourth-century church father and (cantankerous) apologist Epiphanius names them Mary and Salome (*Panarion* 78, 8; *Ancoratus* 60).

2. Fragments of this Jewish-Christian Gospel are all that are extant. This particular fragment is quoted by Jerome in his work, *Against Pelagius*, 3, 2. (See Edgar Hennecke, *New Testament Apocrypha, Vol. One: Gospels and Related Writings*, edited by Wilhelm Schneemelcher [English translation edited by R. McL. Wilson] [Philadelphia: Westminster, 1963], 146–47.)

Righteous."[3] To say that James "was holy from his birth" is to say, in effect, that he was someone who had openly practiced his faith in God throughout his life without affectation. And if he had followed, even at a distance, John the Baptist, we can imagine James as a character whose seriousness in religious matters had lastingly impressed those who encountered it. In fact, he may have been scandalized at first by his brother's ministry and growing reputation precisely *because* he took his faith so very seriously. One brother's reactions to another can sometimes be censorious—and wrong, but for the "right" reasons.

Be that as it may, between the Gospels and the book of Acts something had evidently occurred to transform James and his family's opinion of Jesus, as well as their role among the disciples. We have already noted that Paul apparently attributed this change to an encounter between James and the risen Christ. There is a legend preserved in the second-century *Gospel of the Hebrews* that purports to tell the story of this post-resurrection encounter. This was a Gospel that originated in Egypt among Greek-speaking Jewish Christians and comes to us now, like *The Gospel of the Nazarenes*, only in fragments through the writings of various early Fathers. Although it is legendary in nature, it is interesting enough to quote in full:

> And when the Lord had given the linen cloth to the servant of the priest, he went to James and appeared to him. For James had sworn that he would not eat bread from that hour in which he had drunk the cup of the Lord until he should see him risen from among them that sleep. And shortly thereafter the Lord said: Bring a table and bread! And immediately it is added: he took the bread, blessed it and brake it and gave it to James the Just and said to him: My brother, eat thy bread, for the Son of man is risen from among them that sleep.[4]

The story assumes that James had been present at the Last Supper, where he had made a vow of abstinence. The mention of a "linen cloth" seems to refer to Jesus' burial clothes, apparently given "to the servant of the priest"

3. The five historical books of Hegesippus are lost to us, and what we have of them are what has been preserved by Eusebius of Caesarea in his *History of the Church*. I am quoting from Williamson's smooth, readable translation of Eusebius. (Eusebius, *The History of the Church*, translated by G. A. Williamson; rev. ed. with a New Introduction by Andrew Louth (London: Penguin, 1989), 59.)

4. This fragment comes from Jerome's *De Viris Illustribus* (a collection of short biographies, of which this is the second), in which Jerome cites Origen. (See Hennecke, *New Testament Apocrypha*, 165.)

as testimony of the resurrection. The "eucharist" in the story is reminiscent of Jesus' breaking of the bread with the two unnamed disciples of Emmaus (Luke 24:12–35). Whether or not there is any historical kernel in this version of the appearance to James, the canonical account of the book of Acts simply tells us that James and the family of Jesus were gathered in the upper room in Jerusalem with the eleven disciples before the events of the Day of Pentecost: "These [the disciples] devoted themselves constantly to prayer, with a shared intensity of feeling, together with the women and with Mary the mother of Jesus and with his brothers" (Acts 1:14). It is evident, then, that the brothers of Jesus were, by this time, fully integrated into the nascent community of Christ's followers. We can assume that the resurrection appearance to James, to which Paul alludes, had already occurred.

When next we hear of James in the book of Acts, he has taken a principal role in the life of the mother church in Jerusalem. After Peter's arrest and escape in chapter 12, Peter has little choice but to flee the city. Before he goes on the run, however, he gives final instructions that those gathered in the house of the mother of John Mark should inform James: "And, gesturing with his hand for them to be silent, he related to them how the Lord had led him out of the prison, and said, 'Report these things to James and the brethren.' And going out he went off elsewhere." (Acts 12:17) Following Peter's departure, James is depicted in Acts as the principal authority in the mother church, "the first among equals," and even Peter later in the book appears to submit to his authority and judgment (just as, in Gal 2:12, Paul implies that Peter did not want to risk any disagreement with the emissaries sent to Antioch by James). Quite suggestively, it is James who, at the council of Jerusalem, delivered the verdict concerning the grounds for table fellowship between Jewish and gentile believers in Christ:

> And, after remaining silent, James spoke up, saying, "Men, brothers, listen to me. Simon has declared how God first saw to it that he would take a people for his name from the gentiles. And the words of the prophets agree with this, just as has been written: "'After these things, I will return and rebuild the fallen tabernacle of David, and will rebuild its ruins and erect it again, so that the rest of humankind might seek out the Lord, even all the nations, those upon whom the name of the Lord has been invoked,' says the Lord who does these things, known from an age ago.' *Hence my verdict is* not to cause difficulties for those among the gentiles turning to God, but rather to write them, telling them to abstain from the pollutions of idols, and from whoring, and from anything

strangled, and from blood. For Moses has men who preach him in every city, being read aloud in the synagogue every Sabbath since the times of generations long past." (Acts 15:13–21; cf. Amos 9:11–12; emphasis mine)

We see James once more in the book of Acts, right before the arrest of Paul in Jerusalem. Paul had sought him out and followed his and the other elders' instructions, which were intended to mollify those who regarded Paul as an apostate from Judaism (Acts 21:18–26). It was to no avail, and Paul was taken into custody, nearly losing his life in the violent altercation that ensued. But on both occasions in Acts—the council of chapter 15 and the advising of Paul in chapter 21—we see James as both the preeminent figure in the mother church, one whose wisdom and pragmatism are manifest and respected, and as the mediating influence between Paul's mission and the original Jewish Christian fellowship based in Jerusalem.

The Jewish historian Josephus tells of James's execution (*Antiquities* XX, 9, 1), which occurred between the time of the Roman procurator Felix's death and the coming of his successor, Albinus, to fill his empty post (i.e., sometime in the middle of the year 62). James's martyrdom was a blow to the Jerusalem community from which it never fully recovered. He and others (apparently Jewish Christians), Josephus tells us, were arraigned before the High Priest Hanan ben Hanan and the Sanhedrin, who, taking advantage of the Roman procurator's empty office, found them guilty, possibly of "transgression of the Law," and ordered them stoned to death. Hegesippus, writing sometime circa 180, elaborates on the story (Eusebius, *History*, II, 23). In the latter account, the religious leaders during Passover implore James—who is acknowledged by them to be a "righteous one"—to declare to the crowd from the parapet of the Temple "that they must not go astray as regards Jesus." James boldly declares the opposite and is thrown from the parapet in retribution, whereupon he is stoned and finally dispatched by a fuller with a club. Of the two versions, Josephus's less sensational telling is obviously the more plausible.

Hegesippus, inaccurate though he may be, nevertheless shows us how highly regarded James became in the following generations of Jewish Christianity. His description of an ascetical, devout, even priestly James is almost certainly an exaggeration, but it may also contain some dim memories of the actual man:

[E]veryone from the Lord's time till our own has called [him] the Righteous . . . . [H]e drank no wine or intoxicating liquor and ate no animal food; no razor came near his head; he did not smear himself with oil, and took no baths [cf. Num 6:1–21]. He alone was permitted to enter the Holy Place, for his garments were not of wool but of linen. He used to enter the Sanctuary alone, and was often found on his knees beseeching forgiveness for the people, so that his knees grew hard like a camel's from his continually bending them in worship of God and beseeching forgiveness for the people . . .

We may well believe that James, called "the Just" or "the Righteous (One)," was a man of continual prayer, concerned for his people, abstemious, and possibly "priestly" in his demeanor and even attire. That these were aspects of the serious and devout character of the historical person seems likely, even if Hegesippus can be accused of embroidering some of the facts.

As the gulf between the imperial church and the later Jewish Christian "sects" widened, the memory of the authority of James became an anchor for the latter. No such high estimation of him seems to have lingered among the former. The third- or fourth-century Jewish-Christian *Homilies of Clement* contain two spurious letters addressed to James, one purporting to be from Peter and the other from Clement, bishop of Rome. In them we can see how exalted a figure he had become for the non- (anti-)Pauline churches of Jewish lineage. Respectively, they address James as "the lord and bishop of the holy Church, under the Father of all, through Jesus Christ," and "the lord, and the bishop of bishops, who rules Jerusalem, the holy church of the Hebrews, and the churches everywhere . . ."[5] James has assumed in the imagination of the writer of this pseudepigraphical work, in other words, the position of a "pope," a final authority and governor of all churches.

Perhaps even more remarkably we find in as early a work as *The Gospel of Thomas* this striking logion:

> The followers said to Jesus, "We know that you are going to leave us. Who will be our leader?" Jesus said to them, "No matter where you are, you are to go to James the Just, for whose sake heaven and earth came into being."[6]

5. *The Clementine Homilies*, "The Epistle of Peter to James" and "The Epistle of Clement to James"; from Alexander Roberts and James Donaldson, eds., *Ante-Nicene Fathers*, Vol. 8 (Peabody, MA: Hendrickson, 1999), 215 and 218.

6. *The Gospel of Thomas*, logion 12.

In Jewish literature, the phrase "for whom heaven and earth came into being" is hyperbole, an expression of high praise. On the lips of Jesus, however, it is in this instance highest praise, because here Jesus is personally deputing James as his vicar. Given that this Gospel, and thus this logion, may well be a first- or second-century text, what we have here is an early testimony to the central position James was understood to occupy in the church.

To summarize, then, what we have before us is a sketchy portrait of James, but a suggestive one. He was a devout man throughout his life, so much so that he was known as "the Righteous" or "the Just." He may have been a follower of—or at least inspired by—John the Baptist. Like the Baptist, he gained a reputation for self-discipline, adopting, it seems, traits of the Nazarite vow on a protracted basis (see Num 6:1–21). During at least much of his brother's ministry, he and the other brothers were not followers of Jesus. But, at some point, either not long before Jesus' death or—more likely—after his experience of the risen Lord, James was numbered among the most important witnesses of the resurrection. After the departure of Peter from Jerusalem, James assumed the primacy of the mother church, and became renowned for his wisdom, holiness, and common sense. Even Peter and Paul deferred to him, and it was to James that Paul came for guidance just before his arrest. Finally, in 62, James was put to death, probably by stoning.

Two questions remain: First, in what sense was James "the brother" of Jesus? And, second, was James of Jerusalem truly the author of the epistle that bears his name?

III.

James: The "Brother" of Jesus?

The question of whether or not the brothers and sisters of Jesus were the biological children of Mary and Joseph has had more to do with the church's veneration of the mother of Jesus than it has with his brothers and sisters themselves. Mary's "perpetual virginity" is a belief that is deeply rooted in the traditions of the oldest churches. Christian piety held virginity and celibacy in high esteem from early on. How could it be, then, given the tendency to elevate perfect chastity, that the one chosen to bear the incarnate God in her womb, the holiest of all women and indeed of all humankind, would engage in sexual relations and bear other children after such a holy nativity? If Mary was the most exalted of saints, the pious assumption was that she must have been perfect in every way, especially in chastity. Her role as "the virgin mother" made her a symbol or type of the church (the church was regarded as the "mother" of the baptized and "virginal" in the purity of its faith), and with the development of Mary's iconic status there was more even than her personal honor at stake.[1]

That such a consideration had not been an issue for the writers of the New Testament is evident by their off-handed references to Jesus' brothers and sisters, without once qualifying those terms. For the first generation of Jewish Christians, virginal chastity and celibacy were not regarded as signs of purity so much as signs of calling and consecration, often related to prophetic zeal (as, for example, in the case of John the Baptist).[2] For the New

1. See my book, *The Woman, the Hour, and the Garden: A Study of Imagery in the Gospel of John* (Grand Rapids: Eerdmans, 2016), particularly 28–39.

2. The finest and fullest study of this subject is Peter Brown, *The Body and Society:*

Testament writers, then, whether or not Mary had conceived children other than Jesus was not of great concern. Subsequent generations of Christians, however, influenced by Greco-Roman views of matter and spirit, with the former being regarded as lower than the latter in value, were not so indifferent to the issue of Mary's virginal status. It became increasingly important to see her as the type of the church's perpetual virginal motherhood. The doctrine of her perfect *physical* inviolability was understood as complementing her inner *spiritual* purity.

Not every thoughtful believer in the early centuries accepted the idea, however. One Christian writer by the name of Helvidius, writing towards the end of the fourth century, produced a treatise maintaining that the most obvious (and, it seemed to him, most ancient) way to understand the terms "brothers and sisters" in the Gospels was to take them literally. These were simply the biological children of Joseph and Mary born subsequent to Jesus' birth (and therefore, in Helvidius's view, James would have been the oldest of Jesus' *younger* siblings). The ever-combative Jerome didn't take what he saw as Helvidius's attack on Mary's perfect chastity lying down. He took up his pen and wrote against the latter, suggesting that Jesus' "brothers and sisters" were in reality Jesus' cousins and therefore not biological children of Mary. Jerome's dubious "cousin hypothesis" has continued as an accepted view to this day in the Roman Catholic tradition. There is, however, very little evidence to suppose that the words "brother" and "sister" were used in Jesus' time to mean "cousin."

Another, more plausible view is the one found in the otherwise fantastical second-century apocryphal book, the *Protevangelion of James*, in which the siblings of Jesus are said to have been Joseph's children from a previous marriage. Mary is, in this account, the widower Joseph's young second wife, and Jesus, born of her virginally, is her only child (and so James was, according to this narrative, the oldest of Jesus' *older* half-brothers). This is the view that was supported by such church fathers as Clement of Alexandria, Origen, Ambrose of Milan, Hilary of Poitiers, and others, and it remains the accepted view of the Eastern churches. It is also the reason why, in Christian art both of the East and the West, Joseph has often been depicted as an elderly gray-haired man. The brown-haired, brown-bearded Joseph of popular Roman Catholic art is a later representation.

Men, Women, and Sexual Renunciation in Early Christianity (New York: Columbia University Press, 1988).

Thus we have three early views, all of them claiming antiquity and authenticity, regarding the siblings of Jesus—those of Helvidius, Jerome, and the Eastern fathers. Of these, the first and the last possess more credibility than Jerome's. It is certainly not impossible that the brothers and sisters of Jesus were the children of a previous marriage of Joseph's. On the other hand, long-standing pious tradition aside (a tradition which has, in all honesty, tended to regard even *marital* sexual relations with suspicion and—in its most extreme form—with hostility), the idea that they were also children of Mary, and thus Jesus' younger siblings, is a thoroughly reasonable one.

In this commentary, I will let the matter remain moot and take no definite position on it. But I will, following the usage in the New Testament, continue simply to refer to James as Jesus' brother without qualification.

IV.

Was the Letter of James written by James or by someone else?

In this commentary I will assume that James was, in fact, the letter's author. Some scholars argue that it is a late writing, written under the name of James by some unknown author of a later generation. One can meet with this view in numerous commentaries and study Bibles, too many to list. But, since the arguments for that opinion are well represented elsewhere and can readily be found, I will not repeat them here, but only briefly present my reasons for accepting James as the genuine author.

First, despite tolerable arguments to the contrary, there is no compelling evidence, either internal or external, that the letter must be regarded as a late writing (i.e., between 70 and 100 AD). It can, without any serious difficulty, be dated to the 50s or early 60s.

Second, because the Greek of the Letter of James is quite good by New Testament standards, it has been doubted by some scholars that a "rustic" Galilean, whose first language was Aramaic, could have composed it. But, in actual fact, we do not know at all just how "rustic" James might have been during his adult life, or, for that matter, just how polished or poor (or entirely lacking) his Greek may have been. His hometown of Nazareth, after all, was less than four miles from the cosmopolitan Greco-Roman city of Sepphoris—in other words, within easy walking distance. It is conceivable that James could have acquired a working knowledge of Greek there at some point during his life. If he had shared the trade of Joseph, his father, he may even have been personally involved in the building project that was taking place there while he was a young man. In later life, of course, he lived in Jerusalem, and among those who were members of the church in that city were Hellenistic Jews, whose first language was Greek. If he hadn't already learned it elsewhere, he could have learned Greek through them. Alternatively, if he, in fact, really didn't know a lick of Greek (which seems doubtful), he might have employed a bilingual amanuensis and translator to help him compose his letter. In short, the argument that his Greek is overly polished fails to convince.

Third, the Letter of James appears to be an encyclical epistle—that is to say, it is a letter addressed to all Christians, who are designated in it as "the twelve tribes in the Diaspora [i.e., Dispersion]," in other words, the "true Israel" scattered among the gentiles (compare the words of James, as recorded in Acts 15:15–21). Given what we have already cursorily seen as regards James's influential position among the churches and how he was not hesitant to exercise that influence, it seems wholly in keeping that he could have issued such a general letter. As Martin Hengel noted in an incisive essay on James, "It is the first, indeed, the only early Christian letter that opens with the outrageous claim that it is intended to be heard by all."[1] In other words, it is the sort of communication one would expect from a recognized authority of James's stature.

Of course, a suspicious reader (or scholar) might, in turn, suggest that that is exactly what a pseudonymous author would have *wished* us to believe. That is possible, certainly (in the sense that many other hypothetical notions *might* be possible); but is it necessary to harbor an attitude of suspicion when there really is no warrant for it? In short, there is no firm evidence to lend substance to such doubt. We know that James could have written an encyclical letter, and we have supporting evidence in Acts 15 to suggest that he was influential enough to have pronouncements circulated

---

1. Hengel's essay has influenced my own view of the Letter of James, although I would hesitate to follow him in every particular. He goes into some detail, explaining that the epistle, written by James himself, is a sustained anti-Pauline polemic following the arrest of Paul (i.e., sometime between 58 and 62), and (at least, primarily) addressed to the Gentile Christians of Paul's mission. He highlights seven passages that—to his mind—are direct attacks by James on Paul's character and theology. I believe Hengel is too extreme in his conclusions, and that not all the "evidence" he accrues is convincing. To his credit, he states that he is only engaging in "a 'science of conjecture.'" Still, caveats aside, many of his conjectures ring true enough that, in muted form, some of them will reappear in my own commentary below. Martin Hengel's 1987 essay, "The Letter of James as Anti-Pauline Polemic," can be found, in a somewhat abridged form, in *The Writings of St. Paul: A Norton Critical Edition* (2nd ed.), edited by Wayne A. Meeks and John T. Fitzgerald (New York: W. W. Norton, 2007), 242–53.

to the churches he regarded as under the oversight of the mother church in Jerusalem. The Letter of James fits into that early model of ecclesiastical oversight quite naturally.

Fourth, as we will see in our exploration of the text itself, the epistle appears to engage in a polemic, if not against Paul himself, then almost certainly against a misunderstood or corrupted version of Paul's message. This is nowhere more evident than in the second chapter (the one that so provoked Martin Luther), in which James states flatly that one is not justified "by faith alone," and that Abraham was "made righteous [i.e., justified] by works" (Jas 2:21, 24; compare Rom 5:1 and Gal 2:16). As Hengel proposed, other passages likewise could indicate a sustained polemic that may characterize the whole epistle.

To give but one example, it is conceivable that the passage about sins of the tongue in chapter three might be related—either directly or indirectly—to Paul's well-known penchant for "speaking like a fool" (2 Cor 12:11) and lashing out in angry outbursts against his opponents (e.g., Gal 1:8–9 and 5:12). Christians over the centuries, rightly revering Paul for his greatness on many levels, have tended to explain away such intemperate rhetoric or justify it as "righteous zeal" for the sake of the gospel. We forget, however, that such behavior may not have been considered acceptable by someone as austere as James apparently was. After all, as we can note in his letter, his ethics is in the spirit we hear in the Sermon on the Mount, wherein all "judging" and "condemning" of others is rebuked out of hand.

There is at the very least in James's epistle a direct confrontation with what appears to be a poorly digested Paulinism, one that has misinterpreted Paul's teaching about faith and good works, thereby letting self-discipline slip, "faith" to be perverted into mere assent to doctrines, and inequality between rich and poor Christians to flourish (and one can see, from even a cursory reading of Paul's letters, that he himself had to deal with such distortions of his gospel: "What shall we say then? Should we persist in sin so that grace might abound? Let it not be! We who have died to sin, how shall we still live in it?"; Rom 6:1–2).

Fifth, as we have already had occasion to note, James's moral injunctions have numerous parallels with the teachings of Jesus as we find them in the Synoptic Gospels, and in Matthew in particular. At the same time, these are indeed parallels and not direct quotations—echoes, as it were, of a common body of teaching fully digested and integrated by James into the body of his letter. In other words, one has the impression that James is so close in time and spirit to his brother *that he has no need to quote him word for word*. What we find instead is a shared ethos, imbibed from the source and flowing through James, and practiced in every aspect of his daily existence. As such, he simply communicates it with an easy authority gathered from lived experience. He speaks in the same spirit as his risen brother, and one senses that that is all he believed was required.

Taken together, these reasons for my acceptance of the genuineness of James's authorship may not be persuasive for some, but they are sufficient for me to come down on the side of its authenticity.

V.

The Spirit of this Commentary

If there is a single passage in the Letter of James that can be said to illuminate the essence of the book's overall message for me, it is this: "For the one who has gazed intently into the perfect law, which is one of freedom, and has stayed there next to it, becoming not a forgetful listener but instead a doer of work—this one will be blissful in what he does. If anyone fancies himself religious while not bridling his tongue, but instead deceiving his own heart, his religion is empty. Pure and undefiled religion before the God and Father is this: to watch over orphans and widows in their affliction, to keep oneself unstained by the cosmos." (Jas 1:25–27)

James's chief purpose in writing his epistle, then, is to remind his readers of the characteristics that constitute "pure and undefiled"—that is to say, *true*—"religion." No term in recent decades has been so ill-defined and maligned at the same time as the word *religion*—both by those professing no faith and by those professing faith in Jesus Christ. It may be one thing for non-religionists (or anti-religionists) to get it wrong, either through ignorance or malice, but it is quite another for Christians to think that there is anything to be found in either the Old or New Testament that speaks against "religion" per se. Certainly they can find texts that castigate false religion or negligent and hypocritical religious leaders, but they will find absolutely none that denigrate religion itself.

The term, admittedly, is difficult to define, especially since the study of religions in recent centuries has come to use it as an umbrella word to cover a variety of beliefs—monotheistic, monist, henotheistic, polytheistic, pantheistic, atheistic, animist, and anything else that can fall under its capacious and amorphous shade. For our purposes, the meaning that the term held for James must suffice. The word that he used and is translated as "religion"—θρησκεία—originally meant "fear of the gods," hence "worship" and "piety", and was understood in its practical sense to mean *service rendered to deities, a deity, or the Deity*. For James, as for Jesus, "religion" meant specifically *Jewish* religion, and—as they both clearly taught—it is a religion not primarily about, or reducible to, externals. Before anything else, it must be a matter of the heart. It is about the transformation of the human soul and the human mind: "Draw near to God and he will draw near to you. Cleanse your hands, you sinners, and purify your hearts, you double-souled men." (Jas 4:8)

The teachings and ethics of Jesus were eminently pragmatic in nature, and James is likewise a pragmatist—for him, proof is in the pudding, faith without works is dead, "fruits not roots" are what matter, and doctrine is only valid when it is inspirited by practice. There is no orthodoxy without orthopraxy, and of the two the latter is what will count most in the "day of judgment." That means that any service that is rendered to God must at the same time be a service that benefits human beings, who are made in the image of God, but not to the neglect of one's own self ("keeping *oneself* unstained by the cosmos"). This theme positively dominates the letter, whatever particular matter James addresses. It is the epistle's undercurrent even when it is not explicitly stated. Sarvepalli Radhakrishnan, the great Indian statesman and philosopher, wrote about his own tradition in words that can be easily applied to the mind of James (and Jesus): "Our enjoyment of the world is in direct proportion to our poverty. A call to renunciation in the sense of killing out the sense of separateness and developing disinterested love is the essence of all true religion."[1]

James, then, is tackling a grave misapprehension of what constitutes the nature of Christian religion. It is currently fashionable in some evangelical circles to contrast Jesus with "religion," conveniently undefined and forgetful that Jesus attended synagogue and revered the Temple as his "Father's house." It has also become a cliché in formally non-religious contexts to speak of being "spiritual but not religious," as if these two terms have clearly defined meanings and can be legitimately placed in opposition to one another. But neither of these constructed rivalries (Jesus vs. religion and spirituality vs. religion) would have made any sense to James or to

1. Radhakrishnan, *Indian Philosophy, Volume I* (London: George Allen & Unwin, 1923), 216.

Jesus, both of whom were observant Jews and both of whom taught that religion is primarily an interior ("spiritual") reality.

James's concern is certainly not whether or not one can rightly call Christ's message "religious"—for him, that can never be in doubt—but, rather, whether or not the recipients of his letter can be said actually to be practicing the religion of Jesus or only paying lip service to it. When James reprimands them for a show of formalism masquerading as "faith," for having unbridled tongues, for judging and condemning others, for sucking up to the rich and powerful and disdaining the poor (among whom he numbers himself and all followers of Jesus), and so on, he is in fact striking at a series of manifestations of a single recurrent blight on Christian life: *false religion*. For James, Christ taught *true religion*, "pure and undefiled," and indeed it is visible only in the exercising of (to borrow Radhakrishnan's phrase) "disinterested [i.e., nondiscriminatory] love"—the sort of love Jesus referred to when he said, "So be perfect [which, in context, means 'be perfect' in showing love], as your Heavenly Father is perfect" (Matt 5:48). A "religion" that does not demonstrate active care for "the least" (cf. Matt 25:40, 45) and throws aside self-discipline is in its essence false, impure, and defiled. And no amount of "correct theological opinions" can make it true or clean or, in James's terms, alive.

James is at odds, therefore, with a merely intellectualized religiousness—indeed, with a "theology" that is mostly otherworldly and abstract, that resides in ideas and opinions and goes no deeper, the sort of "theology" that doesn't leave the study or the lecture hall or one's own cerebrations: "You have faith [belief] that God is one? You are doing well. Even the daemonic beings have that faith, and they tremble." (Jas 2:19) His focus is on the things that make for one's inner purification: "But, if any of you lacks wisdom, let him ask for it from the God who gives to all unreservedly and without reproach, and it will be given to him . . . . Every good act of giving and every perfect gift is from above, descending from the Father of the Luminaries, with whom there is no alternation or shadow of change. Having so resolved, he gave birth to us by a word of truth, so that we should be a kind of firstfruits from among his creatures." (Jas 1:5, 17–18)

As noted above, James is a moralist in the purest sense. He clearly regards genuine religion as integrally *ethical* in nature. Mystical experience and doctrinal expertise are barren without moral effort and transformation. There is no distinction between justification and sanctification. Faith is made evident by one's praxis. Again, in words that are meant to hit his readers hard, "faith by itself, if it does not have works, is dead" (Jas 2:17). For James, there can be no equivocation on this point. He means, quite simply, that what is left of one's "religion," sans practical goodness, loving acts, and, in short, the ethical dimension is nothing but a hollow shell, a thing in decay. A mere intellectual assent to a *credo* ("I believe . . .") is not enough. It must become a living thing that bears fruit.

Through his exhortations James seeks to raise "the dead." That is to say, he urges his hearers to awake and abandon behaviors that are redolent of an unrecognized spiritual death. One need only note his recurring "death" language: the unbridled tongue is "a restless evil full of *lethal* venom" (Jas 3:8); the unruly passions cause his hearers to "*murder*" and "fight and wage *war*" (Jas 4:2); the riches of the rich "will eat [their] flesh like fire" on the day of their judgment because, in this life, they "have gorged [their] hearts on a day of *slaughter*" and "have condemned—have *murdered*—the upright man" (Jas 5:3, 5–6). James believes that even among those who profess faith, the seeds of spiritual death can still sprout: "But everyone is tempted by his own desire, being drawn away and enticed; this desire, having conceived, gives birth to sin, and sin fully grown bears *death* as its offspring." (Jas 1:14–15) He concludes his epistle with this admonition: "Be aware that the one who turns a sinner back from the error of his way will save his soul from *death* and will cover over a multitude of sins" (Jas 5:20). And this is precisely what James himself is doing throughout his letter—trying to turn sinners back from their error and cover their sins. He is saving them from death.

"Death" in James's use of the word is, as I have said, primarily a *spiritual* condition, or—better—an *anti-Spiritual* condition. It is akin to the Gospel of John's warning that one is either reborn or else "perishing" (e.g., the oft-quoted John 3:16). "Spirit" is a word that means literally "breath," and it is breath that gives life; thus we have James's peculiar analogy, which to our ears may sound backwards: "For just as the body without spirit [breath] is dead, so also faith without works is dead" (Jas 2:26). Surely, we might argue, he must mean the reverse: after all, works seem to us to be *corporeal*, while faith is regarded as interior and *spiritual*. But, not so, says James. Faith, as he sees it, is a *body* that must be animated, become ensouled, a skeletal framework of truths that must be *enfleshed* and *in-spirited* in order to move and touch and heal those with whom it comes in contact. Thus *works*—visible and loving and reaching out to others, so displaying goodness in action—are what make faith a living reality to those whom it encounters. The shadow side of Christianity in every age has been its all-too-frequent tendency to look beautiful, sound lovely, speak boldly, announce its charitable principles, while meanwhile displaying in its behavior and complicity with the world—"the cosmos" of ungodly hierarchies and falsehoods—the very antithesis of its authentic message. This is true today and it was already true in James's day. To such a condition, he speaks roughly: "You adulteresses, do you not know that friendship with the cosmos is enmity with God? Whoever therefore resolves to be a friend of the cosmos is rendered an enemy of God." (Jas 4:4) And he adds, once again referring to the Spirit/breath of life struggling within us to enliven the body of a possibly moribund professed faith: "Or do you think it in vain that the scripture says, 'The spirit that has dwelt within us yearns to the point of envy?'" (Jas 4:5).

It is precisely this animating Spirit "yearning within us" to which I wish to draw our attention throughout this commentary, implicitly if not explicitly. As we have seen already, and will see over and over again, whenever James puts his stress on *ethics* and *works* in the life of Jesus' disciples, he is in fact stressing the Spirit that breathes that life into them. Here alone, James is warning us, is true religion to be found.

As already mentioned, and as will be addressed throughout this commentary, it appears that James was responding to a misunderstood and misapplied Paulinism, one that depreciated corporal works (and thus ethics) as nonessential to salvation. In principle this was a twisting of Paul's teachings, which—contrary to what Paul actually had intended—mistook "justification by faith" to mean a relaxation of sustained effort to adhere to the moral law. Paul himself, rabbi that he was, had rigorously maintained the moral demands of faith, as every one of his letters demonstrates. A perverted version of Paul's teachings, however, appears to be what James seeks to rectify in his encyclical.

James's historical context notwithstanding, the concerns he articulates in his letter are timeless. His epistle is as relevant in our day as it was in his own, and certainly it is just as important for us to heed as any of Paul's letters. I will be bold enough to mention both here and later that we even need James to temper some of the unfortunate rhetoric we find in Paul, rhetoric that has, for example, unintentionally influenced the various churches' often scandalous treatment of those deemed "unorthodox" in later ages. For some readers, this may be a bit much to chew on—that James implicitly rebukes an intemperate Paul. In response, I would suggest that there's nothing to fear in seeing one apostle correcting another's flaws, if indeed that is what is going on in James's letter. If the church is a fellowship trying to keep pace with Jesus, then both reproof and encouragement should be expected at every level, even at the apex. Paul, for all his greatness, wasn't Christ—and if James felt that Paul, or at least his followers, needed correction to stay in line with the teachings of his brother, then we should see in that an example for us as well. No one stands above Jesus' ethical commands regarding, among other things, the condemnation and judgment of others and giving in to intemperate speech.

For too long we have allowed ourselves, usually without realizing it, to put James in a second-class compartment, unconsciously perpetuating the unwarranted disregard evinced by Luther and those before him who weakened the letter's sharp message by deeming it "disputed"—thereby subtly casting a measure of doubt on its authority. It is time to reappraise such thinly veiled dismissiveness and recognize in James precisely the sort of corrective we most need today. Hence, as I've already indicated, I am calling this "a pastoral commentary."

Our own time may not be marked by any greater moral challenges in the church than was the case in earlier generations, but ours is nonetheless a period in which the ethics of right relations between disciples is being put to the test. This is nowhere more evident than in the nations of the West. More and more, it seems, sincere believers are mirroring the behaviors and moods of the world around them. There is a notable increase in coarseness and loose talk, less patience and charitableness towards those with differing (often doctrinally differing) views, a cavalier tendency to judge and condemn others, a quickness to take sides in quarrels, a defensiveness in matters of material acquisitiveness and a negligence of the poor, and so on—all matters which James addresses sharply. Only by ignoring such ethically unambiguous texts as the Letter of James and the clearest teachings of Christ himself, however, can any disciple behave in such ways and still feel himself or herself "safe" and "without reproach." Against all such self-satisfaction, false security, and spiritual arrogance James sets himself in opposition. In this he imitates his brother's rebuking of the distortions of religion among the professional religionists of his day. The difference is that James is taking aim at the churches of "the Diaspora"—that is to say, the churches or Christian "synagogues" (Jas 2:2) in the gentile world. By extension, as I take pains in my commentary to stress, he continues—as the author of a canonical, that is to say, a perennial text recognized as "God's word"—to take aim at us.

Our churches today must relearn how to be pilgrims in an alien social and cultural environment.[2] Unless the communities of Jesus today live, work, and speak like the Christ they are called to imitate, whatever light they may have will go unnoticed in a world where phoniness is quickly spotted and ridiculed. Likewise, if those same communities live, work, and speak like Christ, they will prove to be "a city set on a hill" and "a light to the world." James's message is a timeless reminder to live the gospel, not just talk or theorize about it.

2. As I argued in my book, *Strangers and Pilgrims Once More: Being Disciples of Jesus in a Post-Christendom World* (Grand Rapids: Eerdmans, 2014).

VI.

Outline of the Letter of James

1:1: Greeting

1:2–27: Opening Exhortations

    a. Faith and Wisdom (1:2–8)

    b. Poverty and Riches (1:9–11)

    c. Trial and Temptation (1:12–18)

    d. Hearing and Doing the Word (1:19–26)

    e. True Religion (1:27)

2:1–13: Denunciation of Bias Towards the Wealthy and the Judging of Others

2:14–26: The Divisive Doctrinal Issue: The Relationship of Faith and Works

3:1–12: Denunciation of Wrongful Use of the Tongue, With Focus on Those Who Would Teach Others

3:13—4:10: What is Required for Friendship with God

    a. Two Kinds of Wisdom (3:13–18)

   b. Either Friendship with "the Cosmos" or Friendship with God, But Not
      with Both (4:1–10)

4:11–5:6: Admonitions Against Judging Others, Boasting, and Avarice

   a. Do Not Judge One Another (4:11–5:12)

   b. Boasting of One's Plans While Neglecting to Do Good (4:13–17)

   c. Warnings to the Rich (5:1–6)

5:7–12: An Appeal for Long-Suffering and Restraint in Speech

5:13–20: The Communal Life

A Note About the Translation
Used in this Book

Throughout this book I will be using the recent English version of the New Testament that my brother, David Bentley Hart, translated for Yale University Press (2017). I haven't chosen it out of a sense of familial loyalty, although that loyalty exists. My chief reason for choosing David's version, admittedly a self-serving one, is its labor-saving benefit to me. It is as painstaking a literal rendering of the Greek original as one could hope to find. It has saved me the trouble of "re-rendering" verses here and there from a less literal translation such as, for instance, the Revised Standard Version (the version I have tended to use in previous books). All the odd phraseology of the original text is preserved, making it both a little strange to our ears, accustomed as they are to the cadences and customary choices of words that we find repeated in most other English versions. As a translation, it is fresh and new, and yet its close adherence to the original reminds us that the text of the New Testament is ancient and therefore removed from us in time and culture, and so, in some ways, it is not really as familiar to us as we are sometimes lulled into believing. It has been a real boon to make use of this work, and I want to thank David for it here.

All Old Testament citations have been taken from the Revised Standard Version.

Commentary

Anyone who undertakes to write a commentary has presuppositions. They may be doctrinal or historical or even linguistic in nature, but presuppositions are always unavoidable. My presuppositions concerning the Letter of James have been indicated in the Introduction above, and they will be elaborated in the comments that follow, but let me set them out again succinctly here so that there will be no mistaking my own take on the epistle.

First, as detailed in the Introduction, I believe that it is the work of the historical James. If I were to give the letter a date, I would suggest (as Martin Hengel does) that it was written between 58 and 62, soon after Paul's arrest.

Second, I believe that the internal evidence points toward its being an encyclical letter addressed to all the Christian communities, or at least to those mostly gentile communities possessing a Pauline legacy. James, at the time he wrote it (and as later traditions suggest—see the Introduction), saw himself as the "vicar"—to use an anachronistic term—of his brother and Lord in Jerusalem, and in that capacity he was responsible for maintaining peace and order throughout the network of communities under the pastoral oversight of the mother church. His role was superseded after his death, but there is little doubt that he was for a short period of time the most prominent figure in the church.

Third, I think it evident even to the casual reader that James is not merely offering general "wisdom" or stringing along a series of platitudes in his letter, but that he is addressing a grave situation of contention and fracturing in at least a significant number of the communities he exhorts. That he can use such words as "war" and "conflict" suggests that the splits were running deep and getting deeper.

Fourth, the one problematic doctrinal issue—the one which underlies the moral exhortations regarding anger, the misuse of the tongue, the abuse of the poor by the wealthy, pleasure-seeking, and selfishness—is the burden of chapter two: the relationship of faith and works to salvation, or (as we know it) "justification by faith (alone)." As we will see, this makes it probable that James writes in reaction to what appears to be others' misunderstanding of the teachings of Paul. I say "misunderstanding" because at the heart of the matter there is evident confusion—mirrored by James himself—regarding what Paul himself meant by "works of the Law." This will be explored more fully in the commentary below, but suffice it to say here that I believe that the confusion was not so much on the part of James as it was on the part of some who believed themselves to be promoting Paul's doctrine. James may have assumed that they were repeating Paul's doctrines accurately—we can't know that—but his warnings to those who would deem themselves "teachers" (3:1ff.) suggest that his words were directed at exponents of Paulinism. Paul meanwhile was out of the way, but his own writings show that he was painfully aware that he had active opponents working within his communities (see, for instance, Phil 1:15–18). Some of these apparent opponents of Paul might have been emissaries sent from James—but, again, we can't know that. What we can surmise is that the unrest that James addresses is related to a version of the Pauline message that James considered erroneous. James's chief concern is, however, not doctrinal, but the moral consequences of a distorted message in the life of the churches—and what he most wants to see is the cessation of open conflict and a restoration of peace and harmony in these communities.

In this commentary I try to see Paul and his followers from James's perspective. If at times the comments appear to cast Paul in a poor light, it is only because there is something to be gained by recognizing that there were notable differences between the church's earliest protagonists. It is not for the sake of taking sides that we should examine those differences, but papering over them, as if everything was sweetness and light between the gospel's earliest messengers, serves no purpose except to perpetuate a legend. I can only aver my own abiding affection for Paul and affirm that his writings are priceless not only for me, but for all Christians. But I could say the same of Peter, and yet the second chapter of Paul's Letter to the Galatians shows us Paul at Antioch coming down very hard on Peter ("Cephas"). Should we love Peter any the less for that? I have my suspicion, though, that many of us have tended to become so used to reading the New Testament through Pauline-tinted glasses that we forget that Peter very probably had his own side of the story regarding those same events at Antioch—and we might even have had sympathy with Peter had we possessed his version to read alongside Paul's. But with the Letter of James, perhaps, we do get something of the other side of the story; and if we can hear Paul's harsh words for Peter in Galatians with a now customary equanimity, we should likewise be able to hear James's reaction to Paul's teaching (garbled though it may have been when it reached his ears) with similar level-headedness. Should we love Paul any the less for James's criticisms? Not in the least. But knowing that there were sharp disagreements even in the imagined "golden age" of the first century might help us deal more realistically with controversies and difficulties we face in today's church.

With those presuppositions laid out in advance, let me mention two characteristics of the commentary that follows.

The first is that I have, as far as I am able, tried to stick to the limits of the theology and Christology of James. I know I have failed in this, becoming speculative here and there. But, by and large, I have tried not to read later theology or tradition backwards into James's epistle. To give one provocative example, if one were able to go back in time and ask James personally if he believed that Jesus was—without any qualification—"God," it's not at all a given that he would answer in the affirmative. Which, of course, is not to say he would necessarily answer in the negative—but we cannot expect from the first-century (or, for that matter, the second- or third-century) writers a clear post-Nicene theology. James, like Peter or John or Paul, stands at the beginning of the tradition that would grow from the seeds the first generation planted. But that tradition at its fullest can't be projected back onto them without distorting the original texts. In this commentary, then, I don't try to exceed the speed limit—and certainly not the speed of organic growth.

The second qualification is that I have tried to keep the commentary as jargon-free and accessible as possible. I have not spent much effort in analyzing the Greek in these pages, although I have written nothing without the Greek text before us. But I have left it to my brother's straightforwardly literal translation, with only the lightest touch in fine-tuning this or that word or sentence myself, to convey what is to be found in the Greek text. I have also kept footnotes to the absolute minimum.

This is, again, a pastoral commentary. It is meant to suggest to its readers avenues that can be pursued which may lead, not only to understanding the text better, but also to application and practice. I don't offer "lessons" or explicit pastoral applications myself; but I do suggest ideas, plainly articulated, that might be picked up and used within our contemporary communities or for one's personal reflection. I would like to think that this commentary is best appreciated as falling within the tradition of *lectio divina*. If it proves useful to those ends, then its purpose will have been achieved.

1:1: Greeting

Ἰάκωβος θεοῦ καὶ κυρίου Ἰησοῦ Χριστοῦ δοῦλος ταῖς δώδεκα φυλαῖς ταῖς ἐν τῇ διασπορᾷ χαίρειν.[1]

[1:1] *James, a slave of God and of Lord Jesus the Anointed, to the twelve tribes in the Diaspora: Greetings.*

That James opens his letter by referring to himself as a "slave" (δοῦλος) may pose a challenge to contemporary sensibilities. The word for us rightly conjures up the unconscionable. In whatever form it takes, slavery is always abusive, degrading, and exploitative—in short, it is the robbery of the lives of others and the stifling of their humanity. But, to understand what James means by adopting the title of slave, we must try to hear it, first, with reference to the historical Greco-Roman context in which he lived, and, second, as slavery having been legislated for the Hebrews in the Mosaic Law.

In the former context, some Roman slaves had the possibility, for various reasons, of gaining their freedom and becoming Roman citizens with full privileges. Many slaves were permitted property and prestige, and were educated and proficient in various skilled vocations. Luke, a Greek physician and a companion of Paul, reputedly the author of the Gospel that bears his name and the book of Acts, may formerly have been a slave—many physicians were. The Stoic philosopher, Epictetus, was born a slave, but was permitted to study philosophy and was already respectable in Roman society before his manumission in 68 AD.

Still, we should be careful not to paint Roman slavery in too bright colors for all that—after all, slaves were owned by their masters. Their very bodies were considered the property of those who had absolute say over

---

1. All Greek citations are taken from M. W. Holmes, ed., *The Greek New Testament: SBL Edition* (Bellingham, WA: Lexham; Society of Biblical Literature, 2014).

their lives. James, using the term for his own vocation, would have been keenly aware of this aspect of the institution.

As a "slave" of God and Christ ("the Anointed"), James is saying that he is not a free agent. And yet we can also presume that he has freely and consciously chosen this service. With his Hebrew background, James would have been aware of the male (though not the female) slave's "rights" under the Law of Moses. Male Hebrew slaves were to be freed after six years of service (although they were not free to take with them their wives and children if the slave's wife had been provided by the master). That is to say, male Hebrew slaves were to be freed unless they *chose* to remain in service to their master:

> Now these are the ordinances which you shall set before them. When you buy a Hebrew slave, he shall serve six years, and in the seventh he shall go out free, for nothing. . . . But if the slave plainly says, "I love my master, my wife, and my children; I will not go free," then his master shall bring him to God, and he shall bring him to the door or the doorpost; and his master shall bore his ear through with an awl; and he shall serve him for life. (Exod 21:1–2, 5–6)

When the Old Testament prophets referred to themselves as God's "slaves" (including Moses himself—see Deut. 34:5), it was with this understanding in mind. It was a service entered into, a conscious decision as well as a vocation, in answer to a call: "And I heard the voice of the Lord saying, 'Whom shall I send, and who will go for us?' Then I said, 'Here am I! Send me'" (Isa 6:8). So James, standing consciously in this tradition, meant by "slave" a firm and willing commitment to *serve*. In an epistle that stresses strict conformity to the teachings of Christ as the standard of discipleship, such an image is appropriate for the one relaying the commands of his master to fellow servants.

It is also to be noted that a slave was not someone who ranked high in the estimation of society. That this term is used in the New Testament, not only by James, but by Paul to designate himself (e.g., Rom 1:1), by Jesus to designate his disciples (e.g., Luke 17:7–10), and even about Jesus himself (e.g., Phil 2:7), is a reminder that the earliest Christians identified themselves with the lowly and those lacking power and influence in society. They saw themselves as *God's* slaves, and that identification lent them an inherent dignity, to be sure; but this slavery also meant they willingly withdrew themselves from seeking after the worldly empire's ideas of privilege and prestige, in order to be a sign to it of another "empire" existing in its midst. The designation "slave" clearly indicated that they no longer "belonged" to the world or (as this translation literally translates it) "the cosmos," but rather they owed their primary allegiance to God and Christ. And if we also note in this something like a trace of defiance against the prevailing status quo, which saw in the status of slaves nothing to envy or respect, we may not be too far off the mark either.

James tells us that he is co-owned by "God" and "Lord Jesus the Anointed [i.e., the Messiah or Christ]." In 2:19 he will confess, as a faithful Jew, that "God is one"; but here he so closely links God with the Lord (κύριος) Jesus that his affirmation of their unity, although it is unspecified as to how that unity is to be understood, is a striking one. To belong to the Anointed One is, in James's view, to belong to God and vice versa. As the "slave" of both, he answers to both as to a single master. This recognition of his earthly brother's exalted position is, we presume, traceable to his conviction that the latter was risen from death and living in the immediate presence of God. As we saw in the Introduction, the claim that James had encountered the resurrected Jesus shortly after his crucifixion was well known among the earliest Christians (cf. 1 Cor 15:7).

James's greeting "to the twelve tribes in the Diaspora" draws on Israelite history—the dispersion of the Jews throughout gentile lands. Here the designation means followers of Christ living elsewhere than in Jerusalem, both Jews and gentile converts. They are, with the mother church in Jerusalem, evidently regarded by James as the legitimate continuation of Israel, symbolized by the phrase "the twelve tribes" (that is to say, "the fullness of" or "the complete" and "restored" Israel). He conceives the churches (or, as he refers to them, "synagogues"—see 2:2) to which he writes as "spiritually" Jewish through faith in the Jewish Messiah.

Also, by "diaspora" we should understand that those to whom he writes are being labeled, in effect, "resident aliens"—strangers in exile. James, then, writes as a "slave" to communities of "aliens." To Roman ears—as to our ears today, perhaps, with our exaggerated worries about refugees and illegal aliens and the supposed "need" to build walls and establish legislation to keep them out—such terms were not guaranteed to be endearing. That early followers of Jesus used such terminology to define themselves was provocative in a society where rigid hierarchy and order was the standard, and in which any provocation that threatened to undermine that standard was met with harsh resistance. Slaves and aliens were, by definition, low on the social totem pole; but Christians embraced, with no regrets, that lowest of levels as their own. Again, we may see something very like defiance in this.

Finally, as we noted in the Introduction, this is an "encyclical letter." To quote Martin Hengel once again, "It is the first, indeed, the only early Christian letter that opens with the outrageous claim that it is intended to be heard by all." James is writing to all Christians, including (or, possibly, especially or exclusively) to all the churches founded by Paul. He is, as he says, the "slave" of God and Christ; but he bears, as paradoxical as that term "slave" would seem to render it, the *authority* to address all without anyone gainsaying his right to do so. If he were not a "slave" bearing the message of the Master to the Master's disciples, he would have no such authority, nor would he possess the right to exhort his readers to observe the basic commandments that he will go on to present in the letter. James claims no originality or authority of his own—he is merely the messenger.

1:2–27: *Opening Exhortations*

What follows immediately upon the address is a series of exhortations, some of which will be repeated and fleshed out more fully later in the letter. In style, the remainder of this first chapter is reminiscent of the wisdom literature of the Old Testament, especially the books of Proverbs and Sirach. And, in fact, James begins by imploring his readers to pray for whatever wisdom they might be lacking. Wisdom, for James, is both a gift available to all whom he addresses and practical in nature. It isn't something mystical, to be attained through some arcane religious practices. Quite the opposite, it's a foundational quality of character, readily obtainable, and the essence of the very this-worldly teachings he imparts. Wisdom is the beginning as well as the end of discipleship, and it is pragmatic throughout.

Is it too much, then, to suggest that, for James, the core of the message Jesus imparted to his followers was "wisdom teaching"? That Jesus, in other words, was the appointed guide to lead people into the paths of God's wisdom? That the discipleship to which Jesus summoned his followers, and the "kingdom" he proclaimed, were wholly centered on possessing the wisdom—that is, the skill—to live in conformity with God? For James, it seems, how one lives before God and among others is the essence of "the kingdom." Without that, as we shall see, faith in the strictly creedal sense lacks ballast.

a. *Faith and Wisdom (1:2–8)*

[2] Πᾶσαν χαρὰν ἡγήσασθε, ἀδελφοί μου, ὅταν πειρασμοῖς περιπέσητε ποικίλοις, [3] γινώσκοντες ὅτι τὸ δοκίμιον ὑμῶν τῆς πίστεως κατεργάζεται ὑπομονήν· [4] ἡ δὲ ὑπομονὴ ἔργον τέλειον ἐχέτω, ἵνα ἦτε τέλειοι καὶ ὁλόκληροι, ἐν μηδενὶ λειπόμενοι. [5] Εἰ δέ τις ὑμῶν λείπεται σοφίας, αἰτείτω παρὰ τοῦ διδόντος θεοῦ πᾶσιν ἁπλῶς καὶ μὴ ὀνειδίζοντος, καὶ δοθήσεται αὐτῷ· [6] αἰτείτω δὲ ἐν πίστει, μηδὲν διακρινόμενος, ὁ γὰρ διακρινόμενος ἔοικεν κλύδωνι θαλάσσης ἀνεμιζομένῳ καὶ ῥιπιζομένῳ· [7] μὴ γὰρ οἰέσθω ὁ ἄνθρωπος ἐκεῖνος ὅτι λήμψεταί τι παρὰ τοῦ κυρίου [8] ἀνὴρ δίψυχος, ἀκατάστατος ἐν πάσαις ταῖς ὁδοῖς αὐτοῦ.

[2]*Consider it all joy, my brothers, whenever you might fall into various trials,* [3]*Knowing that the testing of your faithfulness produces perseverance* [4]*And let perseverance have its operation in full, so that you may be perfect and whole, lacking nothing.* [5]*But, if any of you lacks wisdom, let him ask for it from the God who gives to all unreservedly and without reproach, and it will be given to him.* [6]*But let him ask in faith, not hesitating, for he who hesitates is like a wave of the sea driven by the wind and tossed about.* [7]*For let that man not presume he will receive anything from the Lord:* [8]*A man divided in soul, fickle in all his ways.*

The word "trial" (πειρασμός), which reappears in verse 14, means to "try," "prove," "test," or "tempt." Some commentators argue that the word as used in verse 2 refers to external trials (persecution, for example), while in verse 14 the "trial" or "test" referred to is one of inner "temptation" in the moral sense, which begins with one's desires (ἐπιθυμία), and works its way out with negative consequences for the life of the community (the word will be translated as "tempted," in fact, when we come to verse 14 below). However, I read both verses as referring to the latter, to *inner temptation*, and verses 2 through 18 as dealing with ethical struggles. As we will see, the epistle as a whole focuses on the moral life of the community, so it would seem that there is little reason to regard verse 2 as referring to trials inflicted from outside.

The problems James will address explicitly in the letter are the sorts that crop up within communities, and they originate—as Jesus had warned—in the human heart (e.g., see Mark 7:14–23). So it is that James, before dealing with the serious ethical (and the single doctrinal) issues that concern him, attends first to the hearts of his hearers and to the root cause of their divisive behaviors—what he will later describe as a "war" being waged in their "bodily members" (cf. 4:1). To read verse 2 above, then, in light of verse 14 below makes sense of the other verses that fall in between, as well as those that follow.

So it is that James begins his letter with the subject of temptation. He will tell us later, in verse 13, that temptation or testing doesn't come from God—that "God is incapable of temptation by evil things, and himself tempts no one" (conversely, what it is that God provides will be stated in verses 17–18, as well as in verse 5 above). But temptation, James argues, can nevertheless be a cause for "joy" (vs. 2).

His thinking seems to go something like this. That which is within us, meaning irrational and involuntary desires, require our vigilance—and temptation gives us the opportunity to become aware of their nature. It brings them bit by bit into the light. It is part of the process of coming to "know ourselves," warts and all—and in the ancient world the maxim "know thyself" was first and foremost a *moral* injunction. Such testing of our faithfulness strengthens our resolve to persevere, to become transformed and reshaped, which is the sort of "school of wisdom" the disciple community was intended to be.

The goal or aim of discipleship, James says straightforwardly, is that we "may be perfect and whole, lacking nothing." That daunting word *perfection* really shouldn't frighten us. In this instance it is to be understood in light of Jesus' ethical teaching as, for example, it can be found in Matthew 5:43–48. In that passage, "perfection" refers to perfection in the exercise of love, and the "love" Jesus means is the kind that emulates the non-discriminatory goodness and mercy of God. James's statement in verse 17 below, that "every good act of giving and every perfect gift is from above, descending from the Father of the Luminaries, with whom there is no alternation or shadow of change," in fact echoes Jesus' teaching that the Father "makes his sun to rise on the wicked and the good, and sends rain upon the just and the unjust" (Matt 5:45). Being "perfect" in generosity and goodness, Jesus says to his hearers, is to become perfect "as your Heavenly Father is perfect" (Matt 5:48). What thwart our open-handed, gracious, non-judgmental perfection in love are precisely our inner tendencies or "desires" that move us to be selfish, to judge or condemn others, to speak evil, to mistreat or ignore those in want, and the rest—all those failures, in fact, that James addresses in this epistle.

"Testing," then, reveals our selves to our selves. It shows us what needs to be worked on inside us, what needs to change, what we do not or cannot see until a "trial" unveils it. Then and only then has it the potential to be a "joy" to us, because in the recognition of our distorted desires we make progress in learning how to handle them. Verses 23–25 below will refer to the "perfect law" as a mirror into which we look and see how we truly are, and here we see that our tests and trials have a similar effect.

As already touched upon, for James as for Jesus, God is absolute, unvarying goodness. We will return to this when we look at verse 13 more closely below, but it is important for us to understand at this stage that "temptation" or "testing" is *not* God's doing. It arises solely within *our* selves. James doesn't speculate here or elsewhere in his epistle about the deeper source of our unruly desires. He provides no theoretical doctrine of sin, "original" or otherwise. His is a simple, pragmatic psychology, which locates the problem—as Jesus himself had indicated—within the human psyche (cf. Mark 7:15, 23).

James assumes, in Jewish fashion, that we are individually pulled between good and bad interior urgings. We have innate impulses—tending towards God, on the one hand, and tending towards sin, on the other. The latter impulses are simply acknowledged, not analyzed in any theoretical fashion. In contrast to these inchoate desires, our aim should be to learn, through "perseverance," to mature into ever greater "perfection and wholeness." We could call this goal of mature "wholeness" *inner integrity* or *singleness*, and it is the opposite of being "divided in soul," a state of existence we are warned against in verse 8 and again in 4:8. We are, that is to say, called to move from a state of *interior dividedness*, between good and evil, to one of *interior unity*—what Jesus called "purity of heart" (Matt 5:8) and "purity [or singleness] of vision" (Matt 6:22). For this end to be realized, James says, we need to possess the following qualities: "faithfulness," "perseverance," and "wisdom."

"Faithfulness" is, quite simply, the exercising of "trust." The disciple must trust that God is active within him or her.

But, because there exists within us the interior division already mentioned, our faithfulness is naturally tested. In other words, it is our own inner dividedness that invariably tests us—but God himself does not. Over time we learn how to control the pull of our desires. This is what is meant by "perseverance." James's approach here could be called "stoical," and indeed Stoicism exercised real influence on Jewish, and consequently Christian, thought. But, whatever the background influence of Stoic thought may have had indirectly or directly on James, he presents the development of *perseverance* as essential to one's formation. The disciple works *with* God, in synergy with his wisdom and power, and—although he or she may fall and get back up repeatedly—what occurs through both failure and success over time is an increasing awareness of one's self and the maturing of one's capacity for trust in God.

Finally, says James, if one lacks "wisdom," all one need do is *ask* for it. This is also the repeated promise one finds in the Wisdom literature of the Old Testament. For example, we see it in Proverbs 2:1–5:

> My son, if you receive my words and treasure up my command-
> ments with you, making your ear attentive to wisdom and inclin-
> ing your heart to understanding; yes, if you cry out for insight and
> raise your voice for understanding, if you seek it like silver and
> search for it as hidden treasures; then you will understand the fear
> of the LORD and find the knowledge of God.

Wisdom, in this instance, primarily means the practical discernment, insight, and perception needed to grow in emulation of the goodness of God. As James will say later in the epistle, "the wisdom from above is first of all pure, then peaceable, reasonable, accommodating, full of mercy and good fruits, impartial, unfeigned" (Jas 3:17). It enlightens, corrects, and transforms whatever within us is "earthly, natural, daemoniacal" (Jas 3:15). In this way, *wisdom* guides us, strengthens us, and helps us to *persevere*, so that our *faithfulness* may lead to our perfection.

Once again James stresses the goodness of God. When he is implored, God "gives to all *unreservedly* and *without reproach*." In other words, he does not condemn the unwise but earnest seeker or discourage the struggling or the weak. Rather, he provides continuously without reserve to those prepared to receive. So, although James may stress a "stoical" ethic of perseverance and exertion of one's spirit, he unites it to God's willingness to provide what's lacking in us. At every turn, James reassures us, we can be met by an accommodating God.

And yet, there is an admonition attached in verses 6–8.

Faith means for James a steady trust in God's providence. Even if we are inwardly divided by competing desires—urges that move us in the direction of "sin" (a word that literally means "to veer off course"), on the one hand, and a spirit that aspires to union with God, on the other—we can still place our confidence in the goodness of God towards us ("who gives to all unreservedly and without reproach"). Faith is not, it must be emphasized, a matter simply of "beliefs" or *what* is affirmed as a body of "truths." It is active, ethical, and manifested in "work" or effort. Faith cannot be mixed with indecision, even if it unavoidably will be "tested" by competing desires. In these verses, the faith James exhorts his readers to have is trust in God's goodness *to provide wisdom* as needed—in the words of Proverbs cited above, it lies in our own "inclining" of our "heart to understanding."

What James implies, then, is that disciples are to live *in cooperation* with God, in a synergy of their will with God's. God's will, as James has said, is simple, pure, and trustworthy. Ours is in constant formation, struggling against unruly and inchoate desires. But, with perseverance and wisdom, the goal is for us to cease to be "divided in soul" (literally, "two-souled"). The ultimate aim is to move from inner dividedness to integrity, as we said above. The first step in that direction, James tells us, is to let go of our hesitation, trust in wisdom's availability, and out of that conviction to "cry out for insight and raise [our] voice for understanding." And, then, of course, it is to listen and to keep on listening to the teachings of Christ in order to put them into effect. Only our hesitation stands in the way.

In his exhortation to ask God for what is needed—*simply to ask* and to trust that God will provide what we need to become "perfect" or "mature," James is merely echoing the words of Jesus to his disciples:

Ask, and it shall be given to you; seek, and you shall find; knock, and it shall be opened to you. For everyone who asks receives, and everyone who seeks finds, and to everyone who knocks it shall be opened. Or is it not the case that no man among you, if his son should ask for a loaf of bread, would give him a stone? Or, if he should also ask for a fish, would give him a serpent? If you, therefore, who are wicked, know to give good gifts to your children, how much more will your Father in the heavens give good things to those who ask him. (Matt 7:7–11)

b. *Poverty and Riches (1:9–11)*

⁹ Καυχάσθω δὲ ὁ ἀδελφὸς ὁ ταπεινὸς ἐν τῷ ὕψει αὐτοῦ, ¹⁰ ὁ δὲ πλούσιος ἐν τῇ ταπεινώσει αὐτοῦ, ὅτι ὡς ἄνθος χόρτου παρελεύσεται. ¹¹ ἀνέτειλεν γὰρ ὁ ἥλιος σὺν τῷ καύσωνι καὶ ἐξήρανεν τὸν χόρτον, καὶ τὸ ἄνθος αὐτοῦ ἐξέπεσεν καὶ ἡ εὐπρέπεια τοῦ προσώπου αὐτοῦ ἀπώλετο· οὕτως καὶ ὁ πλούσιος ἐν ταῖς πορείαις αὐτοῦ μαρανθήσεται.

⁹*And let the lowly brother exult in his elevation,* ¹⁰*But the rich man in his abasement, because he will pass away like a flower in the grass;* ¹¹*For the sun rose with a scorching heat and withered the grass, and its flower fell away, and the loveliness of its face perished; thus also will the rich man fade away amid his undertakings.*

There is no form of social division more visible than that between rich and poor. The original church in Jerusalem—James's own church—was aware of this from the outset. Thus we see in the book of Acts that, along with their devotion to prayer, the act of baptizing those joining their body, and "the breaking of bread" together as a fellowship, the disciples also "sold their properties and possessions, and distributed to everyone, according as anyone had need" (Acts 2:44). Again, in Acts 4:32, we read that, in addition to proclaiming the Lord's resurrection, "no one said that any of the possessions belonging to him was his own, but everything was owned among them communally." We are not at liberty to separate the early Jerusalem Christians' devotion to the sacramental, pious, and evangelical aspects of discipleship from their rigorous practice of communitarianism, as if the first three features were considered normative and the last feature not. These early Christians regarded all four aspects of their life as integral. Their communitarianism—or, as it can be called according to the strict sociological definition of the word, *communism*—in turn was clearly rooted in the teachings regarding riches of Jesus himself. Nor are we at liberty to suggest that the Jerusalem community was somehow at fault to take its communal practices to such extreme lengths, because later circumstances in that city reduced many living there to a state of poverty, including the Christian population. Paul, as we know, took up collections to aid the Christians there in their time of need (cf. Acts 11:27–30; Rom 15:26–27; 1 Cor 16:1–4; 2 Cor 8 and 9; Gal 2:10). But there is no evidence that it was the shared life of the Jerusalem church that was to blame for their later hardships. All suggestions that that contributed to their want cannot be backed up with evidence.

Disproportionate distribution of wealth is a great divider between people, as the followers of Jesus knew. Whenever imbalance and unfairness are marks of a given society, it is incumbent upon Christians to rectify that inequality within their own communities (and also, where possible, to work to change conditions in the larger context around them). The concerns of the poor were very much at the heart of the gospel that Jesus had proclaimed (Matt 11:5) and that James in turn taught. Returning, then, to the idea of inner "division" as opposed to "singleness of vision," which we touched upon in the previous section, let us now note the fuller context of Jesus' teaching on this subject in Matthew 6:19–24:

> "Do not store up treasures for yourself on the earth, where moth and rust destroy, and where thieves penetrate by digging and steal; rather, store up for yourself treasure in heaven, where neither moth nor rust destroys, and where thieves neither penetrate by digging nor steal; for where your treasure is, there your heart will also be. The lamp of the body is the eye. Thus if your eye be pure your entire body will be radiant; but if your eye be baleful your entire body will be dark. So if the light within you is darkness, how very great the darkness. No one can be a slave to two lords; for

> either he will hate the one and will love the other, or he will stand
> fast by the one and disdain the other. You cannot be a slave both to
> God and to Mammon.

Without going into detail on this passage, we note briefly that the "division" Jesus stresses here is between earthly riches and heavenly treasure (the latter being a metaphor for the accumulated acts of goodness that are, before God, a person's true, ineradicable "wealth"). It is a division, which is total in nature, between serving God and serving Mammon (a term that refers to riches). Jesus says starkly that a divided "service" simply "cannot" exist. And this is only one instance, among others, of his absolutism in the matter of material wealth.

So James, sensitive to the teachings of his Master, moves quite naturally from a warning against being inwardly "divided in soul" in 1:7 to the subject of external divisions between rich and poor that immediately follows. This is a theme to which he will return again in chapters two and five. In this passage, it should be noted, he sets it within the context of a call for his readers to seek wisdom with faith. That there is a fundamental connection in James's mind seems incontrovertible—just as the communitarianism of the Jerusalem church, adhering to Jesus' original intent, was inseparable from its piety, sacramental life, and proclamation of the resurrection. In other words, Christianity from the outset was a deliberate equalizer between rich and poor within its communities, and this feature was considered part of its basic message. For James, there can be no question but that the application of Jesus' wisdom must, by its very nature, elevate the lowly and abase the rich. In the church, if it is to be true to the mandate of its Lord, there is to be sharing and equality.

The poetic images of the withered flower and sun-scorched grass to illustrate the inevitable death of the rich man echoes Job 14:2 and especially Isaiah 40:6–8. It is an image not only of death but, implicitly, of judgment. It is, in effect, saying: Why are you worried about your riches and your lives? (See Matthew 6:25–34!) You exist with nothingness under your feet, and soon you will disappear into it like everything and everyone must. You, along with all you possess now, are impermanent apart from God. So why not share what you mistakenly believe "belongs" to you during this fleeting life, before you go to face God and are weighed in the balance?

This, indeed, is an indication of the sort of wisdom James expects his readers to acquire.

c. *Trial and Temptation (1:12–18)*

¹²Μακάριος ἀνὴρ ὃς ὑπομένει πειρασμόν, ὅτι δόκιμος γενόμενος λήμψεται τὸν στέφανον τῆς ζωῆς, ὃν ἐπηγγείλατο τοῖς ἀγαπῶσιν αὐτόν. ¹³μηδεὶς πειραζόμενος λεγέτω ὅτι Ἀπὸ θεοῦ πειράζομαι· ὁ γὰρ θεὸς ἀπείραστός ἐστιν κακῶν, πειράζει δὲ αὐτὸς οὐδένα. ¹⁴ἕκαστος δὲ πειράζεται ὑπὸ τῆς ἰδίας ἐπιθυμίας ἐξελκόμενος καὶ δελεαζόμενος· ¹⁵εἶτα ἡ ἐπιθυμία συλλαβοῦσα τίκτει ἁμαρτίαν, ἡ δὲ ἁμαρτία ἀποτελεσθεῖσα ἀποκύει θάνατον. ¹⁶μὴ πλανᾶσθε, ἀδελφοί μου ἀγαπητοί. ¹⁷Πᾶσα δόσις ἀγαθὴ καὶ πᾶν δώρημα τέλειον ἄνωθέν ἐστιν, καταβαῖνον ἀπὸ τοῦ πατρὸς τῶν φώτων, παρ' ᾧ οὐκ ἔνι παραλλαγὴ ἢ τροπῆς ἀποσκίασμα. ¹⁸βουληθεὶς ἀπεκύησεν ἡμᾶς λόγῳ ἀληθείας, εἰς τὸ εἶναι ἡμᾶς ἀπαρχήν τινα τῶν αὐτοῦ κτισμάτων.

¹²*How blissful the man who endures trial, because—having become proven— he will receive the crown of the life that he has promised to those who love him.* ¹³*Let no one who is being tempted say, "I am being tempted by God"; for God is incapable of temptation by evil things, and himself tempts no one.* ¹⁴*But everyone is tempted by his own desire, being drawn away and enticed;* ¹⁵*This desire, having conceived, gives birth to sin, and sin fully grown bears death as its offspring.* ¹⁶*Do not go astray, my beloved brothers.* ¹⁷*Every good act of giving and every perfect gift is from above, descending from the Father of the Luminaries, with whom there is no alternation or shadow of change.* ¹⁸*Having so resolved, he gave birth to us by a word of truth, so that we should be a kind of firstfruits from among his creatures.*

James now returns directly to the theme of temptation. We can speculate how it might relate to the subject of wealth and poverty, which he addressed in the passage immediately preceding this one. But it appears to be the case that these themes are in some sense related in his thinking.

More immediately, though, in the passage before us we glean some insight into James's understanding of sin and how it originates. Compared with Paul's elaborate doctrine of Adam's sin and its consequences for the human race (in turn producing oceans of spilled ink and endless debate down the centuries), which are mainly found in Romans and Galatians, the six verses above are spare and suggestive and say nothing more than what we find in the teachings of Jesus. Though there is no explicit mention of Adam and Eve by James, we can see in his bare-bones description of the origins and consequences of sin the same pattern we see in Genesis 3: *desire* leading through *sin* to a culmination in *death*.

There are two concepts in these verses that are vital in our understanding of James's outlook. The first is James's concept of *God*, which we have touched upon already, and the second is his concept of *human nature* or, we might say, human psychology.

As we have noted above, James's assertions about God stress his goodness. God has no evil in himself, or a shadow side—he is utterly "*incapable of temptation by evil things.*" To say that God is *incapable* of anything may seem to fly in the face of our assumptions regarding his omnipotence. James, however, is not concerned with fine points of abstract theology. He simply asserts that God *cannot* be anything other than good in his nature and actions. God is, in other words, absolute and unalloyed goodness and can only move to do what is benevolent towards his creation. He does not tempt anyone with evil because, essentially, he has nothing in himself wherewith to lure any creature towards evil nor any desire to do so. The sun has no cold, dark spot. God has no evil, dark aspect. And God has no power to change or alter that essential reality of his being. If he is not perfect goodness, he is not God: "Every good act of giving and every perfect gift is from above, descending from the Father of the Luminaries, with whom there is no alternation or shadow of change."

To some extent, this is at odds with many earlier, evolving notions of God in the Old Testament that depict God in such strikingly anthropomorphic terms that he is said, for instance, to "inflict evil" or to "repent" (the latter implying internal conflict in God's "conscience"). James's understanding of God's nature admits no such anthropomorphism at this level. It does, however, fully accord with the nature of the Father as Jesus presents it. Jesus had even gone so far as to correct earlier misconceptions of God straightforwardly, and nowhere more directly than in those teachings we find in Matthew 5:21–48. For example, Jesus taught his disciples to love (meaning to do good to) *all*, even their enemies, *because* the Father loves all, irrespective of their sins and moral impoverishment, and manifests his love through natural provision: "You have heard that it has been said, 'You shall love your neighbor and shall hate your enemy.' Whereas I tell you, love your enemies and pray for those who persecute you; in this way you may become sons of your Father in the heavens, for he makes his sun to rise on the wicked and the good, and sends rain upon the just and the unjust." (Matt 5:44–46) James implicitly echoes this expectation that the disciple should copy the disinterested love of the Father when he writes: "Having so resolved, he gave birth to us by a word of truth, so that we should be a kind of firstfruits from among his creatures." The "word of truth," we may assume, is the wisdom or message imparted by Christ, and, when implanted in receptive souls, it bears fruit. The disciple, in other words, is meant to reflect more and more in his or her life the good nature of the Father on a smaller scale.

But, if the being of God is pure goodness without any shadow of change, the life of human beings—which is drawn from the earth and shares its life with all other living things, and whose existence emerges out of nonbeing—is something quite different in its make-up. James never reflects on how desire (ἐπιθυμίας) has entered the human soul, or how it leads to disobedience and sin. Like the book of Genesis, he simply assumes that desire is naturally part and parcel of human life from the outset (likewise, Jesus never says where, when, or how desire leading to sin has its origin). There is no explicit fall narrative to which either Jesus or James refers, only a pragmatic supposition that every human life will follow the same perennial pattern we see in the fall narrative of Genesis 3.

The reason, James will tell us, that we are enticed to "go astray" (πλανᾶσθε in vs. 16)—some translations render the word "err", "be deceived," "be deluded," "be fooled," and so on—is the result of our "desire." I read "go astray" in verse 16 as synonymous with the word "sin" (ἁμαρτία) in verse 15, which literally means "to go off-course," "miss the mark," or "wander off the path." That it is *desire* that is the instigator of "sin"—causing us to go astray and off-course—is a religious idea shared with many other traditions, including (once again) Stoicism. In Buddhism, for instance, this idea is similar to the second of the Four Noble Truths, which says that our suffering and dissatisfaction in life originates in desire or craving. And it is, of course, desire that tempts Eve to partake of the forbidden fruit in the Genesis story. Like Adam and Eve, every human being has desire as part of their internal make-up. This, in itself, is not a bad thing—without desire the race would not survive—but it can, and frequently does, get us into trouble.

Temptation is, then, according to James, the "test" or "trial" that our own created *nature* (and not God) puts upon us. We live in an imperfect cosmos, one still in development, one not yet as it should be, which has come from nonbeing and the abyss of chaos. The desire we have at our core is a force of nature, a sign of life; but it is life common to every other living thing, and its purpose is survival and therefore by necessity it is self-centered. We cannot help but have this dynamic drive within us (how else would the race propagate? how else would we even feed ourselves?). We are, by the fact of existence, between non-existence and perfect being—the latter being the changeless nature of God.

But it is this *halfway* state of our being, with its inherent earthly drive to survive, that also presents us with the myriad problems of developing attachments inimical to our true welfare, our wanting wrong things, putting our wants before the needs of others, exploiting or hurting others for our own selfish ends, and so on. Desire, in turn, often entices us to "sin" (to "go off-course"; vs. 15), "draws us away" (vs. 14), and leads us "astray" (vs. 16). As *God* is said *to give us birth by his word* so that we can become a kind of firstfruits, *so desire gives birth to sin* and—"fully grown"—leads to "death." By *death*, we can certainly suppose that James means "spiritual" death (dying to God and to goodness), but he also very likely means complete and utter death or perishing, a return in fact to nonbeing. In this, James is similar to the Gospel and Epistles of John, which also starkly oppose the new birth from God to death or perishing. We can speculate how "final" that finality may be, but James starkly puts it before us as one of only two potential destinies.

d. *Hearing and Doing the Word (1:19–26)*

¹⁹Ἴστε, ἀδελφοί μου ἀγαπητοί. ἔστω δὲ πᾶς ἄνθρωπος ταχὺς εἰς τὸ ἀκοῦσαι, βραδὺς εἰς τὸ λαλῆσαι, βραδὺς εἰς ὀργήν, ²⁰ ὀργὴ γὰρ ἀνδρὸς δικαιοσύνην θεοῦ οὐκ ἐργάζεται. ²¹ διὸ ἀποθέμενοι πᾶσαν ῥυπαρίαν καὶ περισσείαν κακίας ἐν πραΰτητι δέξασθε τὸν ἔμφυτον λόγον τὸν δυνάμενον σῶσαι τὰς ψυχὰς ὑμῶν. ²² Γίνεσθε δὲ ποιηταὶ λόγου καὶ μὴ ἀκροαταὶ μόνον παραλογιζόμενοι ἑαυτούς. ²³ ὅτι εἴ τις ἀκροατὴς λόγου ἐστὶν καὶ οὐ ποιητής, οὗτος ἔοικεν ἀνδρὶ κατανοοῦντι τὸ πρόσωπον τῆς γενέσεως αὐτοῦ ἐν ἐσόπτρῳ, ²⁴ κατενόησεν γὰρ ἑαυτὸν καὶ ἀπελήλυθεν καὶ εὐθέως ἐπελάθετο

ὁποῖος ἦν. ²⁵ ὁ δὲ παρακύψας εἰς νόμον τέλειον τὸν τῆς ἐλευθερίας καὶ παραμείνας, οὐκ ἀκροατὴς ἐπιλησμονῆς γενόμενος ἀλλὰ ποιητὴς ἔργου, οὗτος μακάριος ἐν τῇ ποιήσει αὐτοῦ ἔσται. ²⁶ Εἴ τις δοκεῖ θρησκὸς εἶναι μὴ χαλιναγωγῶν γλῶσσαν αὐτοῦ ἀλλὰ ἀπατῶν καρδίαν αὐτοῦ, τούτου μάταιος ἡ θρησκεία.

¹⁹*Know this, my beloved brothers: Let every man be swift to listen, slow to speak, slow to indignation;* ²⁰*For a human being's indignation does not accomplish God's justice.* ²¹*Hence, putting away every defilement and surfeit of evil, receive in gentleness the implanted word, which can save your souls.* ²²*And become doers of the word, and not only hearers, thus deluding yourselves.* ²³*Because, if anyone is a hearer of the word and not a doer, he is like a man observing the face he was born with in a mirror;* ²⁴*Because he has observed himself and gone away, and has immediately forgotten what he was like.* ²⁵*For the one who has gazed intently into the perfect law, which is one of freedom, and has stayed there next to it, becoming not a forgetful listener but instead a doer of work—this one will be blissful in what he does.* ²⁶*If anyone fancies himself religious while not bridling his tongue, but instead deceiving his own heart, his religion is empty.*

In verse 18, James reminded his readers that they had been given "birth by a word [λόγῳ] of truth." But it is by *continuing* to listen "with gentleness"—that is, with humble receptivity—to that same "implanted" λόγος ("word" or, as it can be rendered, "message") that its nourishing power will ultimately have the effect of "sav(ing) your souls" (vs. 21). Only through continuous applied "listening" will receptive disciples reach their goal of liberation.

In verse 19, James sets the stage for the three exhortations that he will flesh out in the brief passage to follow. He will return to these same themes later in the epistle, but here he gives three short, sharp, and apparently interrelated directives. These regard *hearing*, *speaking*, and *anger*: his recipients are, then, to be "swift to *listen*, slow to *speak*, and slow to *indignation*."

Given how much space James will give to these matters in his letter later, we should presuppose that he was addressing actual problems in the churches. It seems unlikely that he was merely giving general advice or offering pithy platitudes. We should assume that there was actual rancor, wrangling, division, inequality, and lack of self-control in the communities to whom he wrote—behaviors at odds with Christ's teachings concerning unity, love, and forgiveness. James is, in other words, really taking these communities to task for actual displays of unruly conduct that have been reported to him. As we might glean from Acts 15:22ff and Galatians 2:12, during the earliest decades of the church the community in Jerusalem regarded itself as uniquely qualified to keep tabs on the goings-on of its daughter churches—including, it seems, those founded by Paul.

James goes on, then, to address these three issues one by one, though not in the same order as we see them listed in verse 19. He begins with a terse comment about "indignation" (verse 20). This is followed, at the heart of the passage, with a few choice remarks on what is meant by proper "listening" (verses 21–25), which for James means, simply and straightforwardly, obedience and active improvement of life in accordance with Jesus' message. And, in verse 26, he comes back to the matter of controlling one's speech—a self-discipline James views as indicative of the genuineness of a person's commitment to follow Christ (as he will address at length in the third chapter). The way James presents these three injunctions shows that he regarded them as interconnected.

We shall look at them one at a time:

Indignation (vs. 20): James says simply that a human being's indignation or anger doesn't accomplish—literally, doesn't "work" (ἐργάζεται)—the justice of God. In the second chapter, we will see that these same two words, "work" and "justice" (δικαιοσύνη), are crucial to his argument there. In 2:14–26 James will make the case that faith requires "works" (ἔργα), and that "justification" (which means to be "proved" or "made righteous/just") compels one to be fully involved in an effort to follow the way of Jesus. We will return to this larger theme of "work" and "justice/justification" in due course, but here in verse 20 we simply note that James means that anger has the damaging effect of erecting a barrier between the justice of God and ourselves. It inhibits our efforts to become just, and as such poses a threat.

One of the most obvious objections to James's warning against anger here would be that even Jesus became angry on occasion—for example, when he drove the moneychangers from the Temple or denounced the Pharisees in Matthew 23. So, it could be argued, there must be times when indignation is justifiable and right. And, in fact, when James comes to excoriate the rich later in his own letter (5:1–5), he will display just such anger himself at the injustices he rails against. In other words, it's a safe bet that he hadn't forgotten his denunciation of anger in chapter one by the time he wrote or dictated chapter five. We can suppose, then, that James might agree, but only up to a point, that anger is not in every instance an evil.

One response to this hypothetical objection is that James—as mentioned above—likely had specific situations in mind, with which he was dealing as directly as he could by means of his encyclical, in which known instances of anger, which could *not* be justified, had already done harm to the Christian community (see 4:1–12). In contrast to whatever forms of anger James was censuring, on those rare occasions when Jesus is depicted as having displayed anger the issues were ones of injustice and exploitation of the lowly. This will be the case for James, too, when we come to his excoriations of the rich later in his letter. Jesus' words and actions had been prophetic in nature, not motivated by self-defense or arrogance or hurt feelings, and had been protective of the mistreated. Likewise, this will be the case when we see James's anger displayed later. It seems evident, then, that James is aiming his words in 1:20 at displays of anger that have other motives than those of Jesus'—as he puts it, they represent the sort of anger that cannot work justice or righteousness. They are a product of "human being's anger" or, as we might call it in our modern idiom, egocentric anger. It is the sort of indignation that comes from a person who is feeling personally thwarted, who denounces specific persons, and whose behavior degenerates to the level of invective, sarcasm, and even wishing injury to someone or some persons.

And, in the New Testament, the one notable figure who—despite his greatness—might be accused of doing precisely that in his writings is Paul. One need only read his letter to the Galatians to see how his indignation, born of worry and stress, leads him to excess (for example, he condemns his opponents with a curse, which he repeats for effect, in Galatians 1:8–9; and he says in Galatians 5:12 that he wishes that those who have demanded circumcision of gentile converts might castrate themselves). One can sympathize with Paul's frustration over what he regarded as an intrusive undermining of the message he had proclaimed, and yet see in it a clear violation of what Jesus had commanded regarding the use of one's words and his denunciation of condemning even one's enemies (see, for example, Matt 5:21–22, 43–48; 7:1–5). We can further suppose that Paul may very well have expressed similar feelings elsewhere in speech and in writings we no longer possess, and that he had garnered a widely reported reputation for having a short fuse—a reputation James could not help but have known about and may have wished not to see emulated among those otherwise indebted to Paul's work. We will come back to this last conjectural point in due course. Suffice it to say here that James's letter may have Paul and his communities in view in more passages than just 2:14–26 below, which deal with the Pauline doctrine of "justification by faith."

Regarding the exhortation in verse 20, we can note that "a human being's indignation" stands in opposition to "God's justice," reminding us yet again that James sees no shadow in God's nature. Self-centered, egotistical anger does not abide in God. It dwells in us because we are susceptible to the imperfect nature we possess, one that comes out of nonbeing into a temporal and contingent existence, one that strives to survive until it must inevitably disappear. Anger is an expression of the propensity we have to make our selves the center of everything. God, in drawing us towards himself, is drawing us into a "newly born" existence wherein we grow to recognize him as the center, and that our lives are connected to everything else that exists. Consequently, we really have no need to cling so desperately to our selves that we lash out or do harm to others. Egocentric indignation, then, is something that cannot by its nature coexist with the goodness of God, if we are to abide in him.

Listening (vss. 21–25): When James refers to "the word" (λόγος) in these verses, he is referring neither to Scripture nor to Christ. It is most likely that he is referring to the Torah (which should not be equated simply with the five books of Moses)—"the perfect law" (vs. 25)—*as interpreted through the gospel of Jesus* (cf. Matt 5:17–20). And he is probably referring to a spoken elucidation of it within the assembly of believers. Before the teachings of Jesus were ever written down, they were communicated orally. "Listening," then, should not be taken as a mere figure of speech in this passage.

"The law" is called "perfect" (τέλειον)—a word that refers to something having "achieved its end" or "goal." Its "end," we might suppose, is that it is the wisdom of God expressed in such a way that the human mind is capable of understanding it—a "perfect (τέλειον) gift . . . from above" (vs. 17). It leads to "freedom" (ἐλευθερίας), which is another way of saying that it "can save your souls" (vs. 21). What it frees us from—saves us from—is the domination of our lives by our passions (such as anger), and it does this by first revealing our selves to our selves (vss. 23–25) so that we can "see" what it is in us that needs to change. Thus we have *looking into a mirror* as an apt analogy for *listening to the word*. "Looking" corresponds to "listening," and the "mirror" that reflects back our true character for us to see—warts and all—is the "word" that is taught.

The Torah is not merely a written text. The word *torah* means "teaching," and in Jewish religion it is presented with interpretive commentary. When Jesus proclaimed his teachings, he was in effect interpreting the Torah to his disciples in a new and fresh way. He extracted from it its essence and spiritual meaning, boldly correcting false notions about the will and nature of God (see Matt 5:21–48), and reinterpreted the "way" that his hearers should follow if they were to be attuned to God's commandments. This renewed understanding of Torah, in fact, was the inspired message (λόγος) and gospel (or "good news") of the kingdom he proclaimed. We can also, perhaps, catch an echo in James's use of the phrase "implanted word" in verse 21 with the parable of the Sower in Matthew 13:1–23 (also Mark 4:1–20; Luke 8:4–15), in which the sower sows "the word (λόγος) of the kingdom." "The word of the kingdom" is the Torah as newly corrected, reinterpreted, and imparted by Jesus. It is the "good news" and also "the perfect law . . . of freedom." For James, these are one and the same. The law is not the antithesis of the gospel. Rightly expounded, it *is* the gospel.

However, before ever we can take it in deeply, we must put "away every defilement and surfeit of evil." What makes us receptive, in other words, is to remove from our lives the most obvious barriers to our receptivity (here, again, we may be reminded of the parable of the Sower, in which the condition of the ground upon which the seed is sown determines the nature of the resulting growth). James is unequivocal: moral effort precedes serious discipleship. It is the same prerequisite Jesus preached at the outset of his ministry: "Repent." The word "repent"—μετάνοια—literally means to "change [one's] thoughts." James tells us that what such internal change entails is the uprooting of whatever things in our lives contrast with the aspiration to live according to Christ's teachings.

James's analogy of the mirror for the word, reflecting our true "faces" back to us, reminds us of Paul's understanding of the role the Law plays, as he describes it in his Letter to the Romans: "I did not know sin except through Law; for I did not even know about covetousness except that the

Law said, 'You shall not covet." (Rom 7:7) But, whereas Paul goes on to *contrast* law and gospel, James instead holds them in *harmony*: "For the one who has gazed intently into the perfect law, which is one of freedom, and has stayed there next to it, becoming not a forgetful listener *but instead a doer of work*—this one will be blissful in what he does" (vs. 25). Contrast James's simple affirmation that one can "do" the word (by which he means the Torah as filtered through Jesus' gospel) with Paul's record of anguish, from which only the gospel—which he depicted as being in stark contradistinction to the law—could save him: "Thus I discover the law that, when I am desirous of doing the good, the evil presents itself to me. For I delight in God's Law according to the inner man, but I see a different law in my bodily members warring against the Law of my mind and taking me captive by the law of sin that is in my members. I am a man in torment . . ." (Rom 7:21–24a). For Paul, when the Law reveals himself to himself, it condemns him—he experiences "torment" in consequence. But for James, far from being a source of torment, when the Law reveals ourselves to ourselves, it indicates what we should work to change so that we can better follow Jesus' way. It becomes, in other words, a useful vehicle in our attainment of freedom (ἐλευθερίας).

There is little need to observe again how very different James and Paul are in their understanding of law and gospel—the two views have their similarities, as noted, but their basic assumptions of what constitutes the gospel are dissimilar. We accept that the New Testament holds these diverse views together within a single canon, but they cannot be entirely reconciled (as Luther recognized). Of the two views, James appears to stand closer to the message of Jesus as we find it expressed in the Synoptic Gospels. He seems to be particularly in accord with Matthew. On a positive note, it might behoove us to regard James as a counterbalance to Paul's (not always consistent) tendency to separate—to the point of opposition—law and Jesus' gospel. Law, as James sees it, does not exist to condemn us or drive us to despair. As interpreted spiritually by Jesus, it reveals our flaws in order that we can cooperate with the work of God—so that, if we are not "forgetful listeners," we can become "doers of [good] work." We can take our cue, perhaps, from the fact that the canon implicitly keeps James and Paul in tension, without offering any neatly fabricated resolution. James and Paul are not mutually exclusive, but complementary. We can hold on to the tension, without pitting one against the other (which Luther could not do), assuming we are flexible in our own thinking.

Speech (vs. 26): James's exhortation in verse 26 concerning the tongue sets the stage for his longer exhortation of 3:1–12. Like Jesus, James is particularly concerned with the abuse of speech (see, for example, Matt 12:33–37; 15:11). Jesus had taught his hearers that "by your words you shall be vindicated, and by your words you shall be condemned." James echoes this strong assertion by stating that the one who does not bridle or restrain his tongue is practicing an "empty" or "futile" religion (θρησκεία)—indeed, is deluding himself or herself. A person may "feel good" about his religious devotion and come away from it with a sense of contentment and edification. But if he goes on to use his tongue in the many ways it can hurt, mislead, and demean others, his feelings of personal "edification" are delusional. In other words, whatever other efforts one may be putting into the exercise of religion—we could say, devotionally, prayerfully, philanthropically, liturgically, by maintaining the orthodoxy of one's doctrines—all these amount to little or no worth if one cannot refrain from gossip, slander, backbiting, verbal abuse, condemnation of others, and so on. This will be, as noted above, expanded upon in chapter three. But I will note in passing here—given the pastoral intention of this commentary—that the tongue can be taken as a euphemism not only for spoken speech but also for any form of communication, including the keyboard and the pen. We will come back to all this when we look at 3:1–12.

With the mention of religion in this verse, which states what true religion *is not*, we are led directly to the following verse, which tells us what it *is*.

e. *True Religion (1:27)*

²⁷ θρησκεία καθαρὰ καὶ ἀμίαντος παρὰ τῷ θεῷ καὶ πατρὶ αὕτη ἐστίν, ἐπισκέπτεσθαι ὀρφανοὺς καὶ χήρας ἐν τῇ θλίψει αὐτῶν, ἄσπιλον ἑαυτὸν τηρεῖν ἀπὸ τοῦ κόσμου.

²⁷*Pure and undefiled religion before the God and Father is this: to watch over orphans and widows in their affliction, to keep oneself unstained by the cosmos.*

COMMENTARY

Just as the final word in vs. 26 is θρησκεία (religion), so θρησκεία is the first word of v. 27 in the Greek text. It appears obvious from the juxtaposed repetition that the reader is intended to note the sharpness of the contrast between what is and what is not indicative of authentic religion. We have discussed at length the topic of religion in the Introduction above, but here a few additional comments might be appropriate.

It is important, in understanding James's Greco-Roman and Jewish context, to observe that "religion" referred primarily to practical observance. It was not something that stood apart, but was seamlessly interwoven with every other aspect of ancient life, whether Jewish or pagan. There was no separate sphere for politics and another for religion. Everyone's daily life involved religious observances, from how and what one ate to the cleanliness of one's house to the offerings one made devotionally to the blessings and curses one might entreat. In practical terms, it was a thoroughly religious world; and even those whose cynicism about religion was known and tolerated, cooperated nonetheless in its public performance. It would have been viewed as uncivil (and even treasonous where the Roman imperial cult was concerned) not to do so.

We should likewise note that religion for James meant specifically the Jewish religion. As we might gather from Acts 15, the issue for the early church was not how to accommodate Jews within "Christianity," but rather how to accommodate gentile believers in Jesus the Messiah within this new Jesus-centered Jewish fellowship. What that entailed was to insist that gentile believers agree to a few essentials of outward Jewish practice: "to abstain from the pollutions of idols, and from whoring, and from anything strangled, and from blood" (Acts 15:20; also 15:29). Significantly, Acts tells us that it was, in fact, James who pronounced this "verdict" (κρίνω) concerning outward observances (Acts 15:19). It is also probable that this isn't far removed from James's assertion above that one should "keep oneself unstained by the cosmos." Abstention from idolatry (meaning anything pertaining to pagan rites) and sexual immorality, and observing certain Jewish dietary restrictions, the violation of which would break table fellowship between Jewish and gentile followers of Christ, could certainly be what James has in mind when he exhorts his readers to remain "unstained."

The term "cosmos" (κόσμος), usually translated "world," suggests a broader concept than merely human "society" or "culture." Although we will come back to what "the cosmos" signified for James (and also John) when we discuss 4:1–10, it is worth noting here that it did not convey the

61

reduced perception we have today when we use the (decidedly non-spiritual) word "secular." Rather, the ancient concept of "cosmos" was that of a hierarchical reality, comprehensive both of human society, order, empire, and peoples, and also of the transcendent and chthonic realms of various spiritual beings and gods. James's warning to stay "unstained," then, is similar to Paul's warning in 1 Corinthians 10:20c–21, explaining why it is that Christians should not take part in pagan civic sacrifices: "I do not intend you to become communicants of daemonic beings. You cannot drink from the cup of the Lord and the cup of daemonic beings; you cannot partake of the table of the Lord and the table of daemonic beings." Like Paul's warning, James's warning is not just "spiritual" in nature, dealing only with one's interior life and therefore hidden from public view. Instead, the admonition is quite pragmatic and dealing with outward behavior as well. While his primary concern is unquestionably "spiritual" in kind, he knows that whatever one does bodily *is* spiritual.

But, that said, James is not merely advocating the replacement of one form of outward observance with another. He knew very well that outward observances do not constitute the soul of religion. No doubt James regarded Jesus as having inaugurated "the new covenant" prophesied by Jeremiah:

> Behold, the days are coming, says the LORD, when I will make a new covenant with the house of Israel and the house of Judah, not like the covenant which I made with their fathers when I took them by the hand to bring them out of the land of Egypt, my covenant which they broke, though I was their husband, says the LORD. But this is the covenant which I will make with the house of Israel after those days, says the LORD: I will put my law within them, and I will write it upon their hearts; and I will be their God, and they shall be my people. And no longer shall each man teach his neighbor and each his brother, saying, "Know the LORD," for they shall all know me, from the least of them to the greatest, says the LORD; for I will forgive their iniquity, and I will remember their sin no more. (Jer 31:31–34)

In Jeremiah's prophecy, the new covenant was no longer to be an "outward" law imposed on the people from above, but rather it would be a matter of the heart, "within them . . . [and written] upon their hearts"—meaning that each person would "know the Lord" and his law at a level far deeper than mere outward observance. Externalism was to give way to "pure and undefiled religion," to use James's terms, an internal "knowing." One is reminded here of Jesus' words to the Samaritan Woman in John 4:23–24: "But an hour comes, and now is, when the true worshippers will worship the Father in spirit and truth; for indeed the Father looks for those worshipping him so; God is spirit, and it is necessary that those worshipping worship in spirit and truth."

Jesus had castigated the Jewish religious leaders of his day on precisely these grounds: "[B]y your tradition you have made the word of God powerless. You charlatans, Isaiah prophesied well concerning you when he said, 'This people honors me with their lips, but their heart is far away from me; and they worship me vainly, teaching doctrines that are the dictates of men.'" (Matt 15:6b–9) In place of religion merely considered legitimate if one kept to the external rules and practices, Jesus adamantly insisted on a religion of the heart:

> And, calling the crowd forward, he said to them, "Listen and understand: It is not what goes into the mouth that defiles a man, but what comes out of the mouth—this defiles the man." Then, approaching, the disciples say to him, "Are you aware that the Pharisees who heard this saying were scandalized?" But in reply he said, "Every plant that my heavenly Father did not plant shall be uprooted. Leave them: They are blind guides to the blind; and if a blind man guides a blind man both will fall into a pit." But in reply Peter said to him, "Explain the parable to us." But he said, "Are you also so unable to understand? Do you not grasp that everything entering the mouth passes on to the bowels and is expelled into a latrine? But the things that come out of the mouth emerge from the heart, and those defile the man. For from the heart emerge wicked thoughts, murders, adulteries, whorings, thefts, perjuries, blasphemies. These are the things that defile a man; but to eat with unwashed hands does not defile a man." (Matt 15:10–20)

These words of Jesus remind us of James's equally strong words regarding the tongue in 1:26, that not to restrain the tongue is tantamount to reducing one's own religion to futility. They also tell us that religion, to be legitimate in the eyes of God, must be rooted deeply in the human heart.

So, when it comes to legitimate externals, what are the true outward signs that one is truly religious—that his or her religion is "pure and undefiled"? It is not legal observances, as Jesus made clear, which reveal nothing about the sincerity of the person who performs them. A surer indicator of genuineness, as we saw in verse 26, is how a person uses (or, better, does not use) his or her tongue. The other indicator, which verse 27 stresses, is practical charity to those who most need it.

James specifically refers to the care of orphans and widows. These represent the most needy persons in his society, who—having no father or husband—are without means and face utter destitution. No follower of Christ, James is insisting, can look at those in need and turn away and yet call himself or herself a worshipper of God the Father (again, taking us back to the indiscriminate love shown by the Father, who is our paradigm, as Jesus presents him in Matt 5:43–48).

The final parable of Jesus in Matthew's gospel (25:31–46), often referred to as "the parable of the Judgment of the Nations," places this great concern for the most needy at the very center of Christ's message. Identifying his very person with the "stranger," the "naked," the "ill," and those in "prison," Jesus says that those who care or refuse to care for such as these are indirectly caring for or neglecting him. This, Jesus says, is what will determine how his followers are to be judged: "'Amen, I tell you, inasmuch as you did it to one of the least of these my brothers, you did it to me. . . . Amen, I tell you, inasmuch as you did not do it to one of the least of these my brothers, neither did you do it to me . . .' And these will go to the chastening of that Age, but the just to the life of that Age." (Matt 25:40, 45–46) James may specify widows and orphans, rather than the stranger, the unclothed, the sick, and those in prison, but the overall meaning is the same. To neglect anyone in need, within the church or outside it, is to neglect Christ and to reject authentic religion—regardless of what else one might do "religiously."

In today's world, we can and should apply this to how we respond to immigrants, refugees, the homeless, those without adequate healthcare, those in prison, and so on. No excuses, no phony distinctions between "deserving" and "undeserving" persons, no refusal to assist those of other faiths or other ethnicities or those who frighten us can be regarded by the disciple of Jesus as anything other than intentional neglect. Either we take our "God and Father" as the paradigm for our actions in the world or we do not. There is no middle position. But, if we do not, we should be honest enough to stop playing at being "religious." *False* religion, which is uncaring and inactive religion, really is—to borrow Marx's term—an "opiate" or, as James called it back in verse 26, a delusion. It is also, as we shall soon see, a *dead* faith: "So also faith by itself, if it does not have works, is dead" (Jas 2:17).

COMMENTARY

2:1-13: Denunciation of Bias Towards the Wealthy and the Judging of Others

²·¹ Ἀδελφοί μου, μὴ ἐν προσωπολημψίαις ἔχετε τὴν πίστιν τοῦ κυρίου ἡμῶν Ἰησοῦ Χριστοῦ τῆς δόξης; ² ἐὰν γὰρ εἰσέλθῃ εἰς συναγωγὴν ὑμῶν ἀνὴρ χρυσοδακτύλιος ἐν ἐσθῆτι λαμπρᾷ, εἰσέλθῃ δὲ καὶ πτωχὸς ἐν ῥυπαρᾷ ἐσθῆτι, ³ ἐπιβλέψητε δὲ ἐπὶ τὸν φοροῦντα τὴν ἐσθῆτα τὴν λαμπρὰν καὶ εἴπητε· Σὺ κάθου ὧδε καλῶς, καὶ τῷ πτωχῷ εἴπητε· Σὺ στῆθι ἢ κάθου ἐκεῖ ὑπὸ τὸ ὑποπόδιόν μου, ⁴ οὐ διεκρίθητε ἐν ἑαυτοῖς καὶ ἐγένεσθε κριταὶ διαλογισμῶν πονηρῶν; ⁵ ἀκούσατε, ἀδελφοί μου ἀγαπητοί. οὐχ ὁ θεὸς ἐξελέξατο τοὺς πτωχοὺς τῷ κόσμῳ πλουσίους ἐν πίστει καὶ κληρονόμους τῆς βασιλείας ἧς ἐπηγγείλατο τοῖς ἀγαπῶσιν αὐτόν; ⁶ ὑμεῖς δὲ ἠτιμάσατε τὸν πτωχόν. οὐχ οἱ πλούσιοι καταδυναστεύουσιν ὑμῶν, καὶ αὐτοὶ ἕλκουσιν ὑμᾶς εἰς κριτήρια; ⁷ οὐκ αὐτοὶ βλασφημοῦσιν τὸ καλὸν ὄνομα τὸ ἐπικληθὲν ἐφ' ὑμᾶς; ⁸ Εἰ μέντοι νόμον τελεῖτε βασιλικὸν κατὰ τὴν γραφήν Ἀγαπήσεις τὸν πλησίον σου ὡς σεαυτόν, καλῶς ποιεῖτε· ⁹ εἰ δὲ προσωπολημπτεῖτε, ἁμαρτίαν ἐργάζεσθε, ἐλεγχόμενοι ὑπὸ τοῦ νόμου ὡς παραβάται. ¹⁰ ὅστις γὰρ ὅλον τὸν νόμον τηρήσῃ, πταίσῃ δὲ ἐν ἑνί, γέγονεν πάντων ἔνοχος. ¹¹ ὁ γὰρ εἰπών· Μὴ μοιχεύσῃς εἶπεν καί· Μὴ φονεύσῃς· εἰ δὲ οὐ μοιχεύεις φονεύεις δέ, γέγονας παραβάτης νόμου. ¹² οὕτως λαλεῖτε καὶ οὕτως ποιεῖτε ὡς διὰ νόμου ἐλευθερίας μέλλοντες κρίνεσθαι. ¹³ ἡ γὰρ κρίσις ἀνέλεος τῷ μὴ ποιήσαντι ἔλεος· κατακαυχᾶται ἔλεος κρίσεως.

²·¹My brothers, hold to the faith of our Lord of glory, Jesus the Anointed, without any respecting of persons. ²For if a man were to enter your synagogue with gold on his fingers and in splendid attire, and a destitute man in begrimed attire were also to enter, ³And you were to look at the one wearing the splendid attire and say,"Here, be finely seated," and were to say to the destitute man, "Stand over there" or "Seat yourself below my footstool," ⁴Have you not discriminated among yourselves, and become judges whose deliberations are wicked? ⁵Listen, my beloved brethren: Has not God chosen the destitute within the cosmos, as rich in faithfulness and as heirs of the Kingdom he has promised to those who love him? ⁶But you have dishonored the destitute man. Do not the rich oppress you, and haul you into law courts as well? ⁷Do they not blaspheme the good name that has been invoked upon you? ⁸Now, if you fulfill what, according to scripture, is a royal law—"You shall love your neighbor as

yourself"—you are doing well; ⁹*But if you are respecters of persons you are committing a sin, being convicted by the Law as transgressors.* ¹⁰*For whoever keeps the whole Law, yet falters in one thing, has become answerable for everything.* ¹¹*For he who has said, "Do not commit adultery" also said, "Do not commit murder." Now, if you do not commit adultery yet do commit murder, you have become a transgressor of Law.* ¹²*Speak and act like persons about to be judged by a Law of freedom.* ¹³*For the judgment on the one who has shown no mercy will be merciless; mercy triumphs over judgment.*

As mentioned in our discussion of 1:9–11 above, the Jerusalem community, over which James presided, practiced a form of "communism" (cf. Acts 2:44; 4:32). The ideal was that there should be equality within the church through the sharing of goods of Christ's followers—an ideal that Paul extended even to parity between entire Christian communities (see 2 Cor 8:14–15). With this as their communal paradigm, then, there should be no disparagement of the poor or deference to the rich among Christ's followers. This is precisely what James is saying in our present passage. Everyone is to be treated as an equal within the community; and God, he says, has partiality for the poor (verse 5).

James invokes the Law in verses 9–13. Underlying the Christian ideal of nondiscrimination between rich and poor is the Law itself: "But if you are respecters of persons you are committing a sin, being convicted by the Law as transgressors" (2:9). In the Law, judges were forbidden to show partiality either to rich or poor in their adjudications (Exod 23:3; Lev 19:5; Deut 16:19). The *Midrash Tannaim*, a collection of the opinions and interpretations of rabbinic sages who lived between 10 and 220 AD, contains an explanation of Deuteronomy 16:19 that is strikingly similar to the words of James in 2:2–5 above: "Do not say this one is rich while this one is poor . . . this one [qualified yet destitute] should sit beneath [me], and do not have it that the poor stand and the rich sit . . . God stands with the poor and not with those who oppress them."² James's words, then, share a common Jewish legal outlook. His Jewishness is further underscored in verse 2, in which he refers to the Christian gathering as a συναγωγή—a "synagogue."

2. Cited in *The Jewish Annotated New Testament* (New York: Oxford University Press, 2011), 430.

James's harsh indictment of the rich in verses 6–7, an indictment that will become even harsher in chapter five, indicates that the majority of Christian disciples were not among that class. And verse 5, as already noted, is clear in its affirmative appraisal of those in humbler circumstances: "Has not God *chosen* [ἐξελέξατο] the destitute within the cosmos, as rich in faithfulness and as heirs of the Kingdom he has promised to those who love him?" It is, in fact, the rich who oppress the Christian synagogues and drag them to the law courts on various pretexts (vs. 6).

It is possible that the term "the rich" (οἱ πλούσιοι) in this case refers primarily to rival Jewish communities. In general, Jews throughout the Roman world were established and prosperous, their religion protected by Roman law. But these also at times regarded the followers of Jesus—the latter with their acceptance of uncircumcised gentile converts—as distasteful and religiously deviant. The rivalry, as we know, grew bitter, as we can see by merely skimming the book of Acts and also such early patristic writings as, say, *The Martyrdom of Polycarp* (XIII,1). When James states that the rich "blaspheme the good name that has been invoked upon you," the "good name" he means is undoubtedly that of "Jesus the Anointed" (vs. 1). Jesus' name, with the addition of the messianic title, was a main source of contention between Jesus' followers and the Jews who didn't confess him.

Still, James is less concerned with the contention existing outside the community than he is with the twin problems of showing partiality towards the affluent and despising the destitute within it. In dealing with these internal difficulties, he doesn't hesitate to make three related points, each of which is uncompromising and brooks no argument from his hearers.

First, the "royal law" is not dispensable (vs. 8): James states positively that to fulfill the "royal law"—"You shall love your neighbor as yourself"— is to "do well." Not to do so, as verse 9 states, is "sin" and "transgression." In short, it is to dispense with the Law altogether (see the second point below).

The phrase "royal law" can be translated "law of the kingdom"—and, in verse 5, we already have a reference to "the kingdom (of God)." To love one's neighbor as oneself, which is an imperative from the Law of Moses (Lev 19:18), was declared by Jesus to be one of the two central commandments that together make the linchpin upon which the entire Torah and all the words of the prophets turn:

> And one of them who was a lawyer, testing him, posed him the question, "Teacher, what is the great commandment in the law?" And he said to him, "You shall love the Lord your God with all

your heart and with all your soul and with all your reason. This is
the great and first commandment. The second is like it: You shall
love your neighbor as yourself. All the Law and the prophets de-
pend upon these two commandments." (Matt 22:35–40)

Again, it is important to note that in the passage above from Matthew, and
also in the Letter of James, the heart of the gospel is one and the same as
the heart of the Law. To love one's neighbor as oneself, then, is "a law of the
kingdom" that must not be ignored—an imperative that must be scrupu-
lously observed.

*Second, to break one of the moral commandments is to break the entire
Law of God (verses 10–13):* Here the Law is referred to as "a Law of freedom" (νόμου ἐλευθερίας). Why? Because the Law prohibits the oppression
of others, and its message—as interpreted by Jesus, especially—is a word
of liberation. James says that it is this aspect of the Law that will determine
our judgment (again, see Matt 25:31–46!). To show *mercy* (vs. 13) to the
disadvantaged—to uplift them, to share their burdens, to help provide for
their needs—is therefore what will give victory over judgment when that
day comes when our lives are weighed.

Where James is at his toughest is in verse 10: "For whoever keeps
the whole Law, yet falters in one thing, has become answerable for *everything*"—meaning, "answerable for the entirety of the Law." He cites two of
the moral laws of the Ten Commandments, the one forbidding murder and
the other forbidding adultery, to make the case that it isn't by keeping *most*
of the particulars but *all* of the particulars that is required. James, like the
other writers of the New Testament, strictly adheres to the *moral* directives
of the Torah. Ceremonial and civic laws, by comparison, are devalued, following the example set by Jesus; but the moral injunctions remain in place
and indeed are stressed and even intensified (see, for instance, Matt 5:20).
So it is that, when James says that one is to keep "the whole Law" (ὅλον
τὸν νόμον), he means the moral essentials of it—the non-negotiable and
perennial heart of it, the summation of which is Jesus' "royal laws" to love
God and neighbor. To "falter in *one thing*"—in this case, by not showing
sufficient love and mercy to the poor—is to break *all* the Law and thus *all* its
interrelated commandments. To deny one of these laws is, in effect, to deny
the One who gave it; and to deny him is to deny the whole.

But that still isn't the toughest of James's three points. The next one is
even more severe yet:

Third, to be "respecters of persons" and not to demonstrate mercy is akin to "murder" (vss. 9, 11, 13): James's indictment is implicit, but impossible to miss, and it is his most cutting assertion. The reason he says, in the unsubtle way that he says it, that "he who has said, 'Do not commit adultery' also said, 'Do not commit murder,'" is because he wants his hearers to recognize that their partiality to the rich and powerful, while disdaining or disregarding the humble, is tantamount to "murdering" the neighbor. "Now, if you do not commit adultery *yet do commit murder*, you have become a transgressor of Law"—those words are like a hammer blow to the complacent, the smug, the self-assured, and the blissfully oblivious. If you dishonor or ignore the needy, humble, lowly, and deprived, you are—knowingly or unknowingly—*killing* them.

This isn't just a peculiarity of James's. We see similar tough analogies elsewhere in the New Testament. For example, in 1 John 3:15, we read the following indictment of those who hate others: "Everyone who hates his brother is a murderer, and you know that no murderer has the life of the Age abiding in him." And Jesus comes close to equating anger and condemnation directed at others with murder in Matthew 5:21–26: "You have heard that it was said to those of ancient times: 'You shall not commit murder; and whoever commits murder shall be liable to judgment.' Whereas I say to you that everyone who becomes angry with his brother shall be liable to judgment . . . ." (Matt 5:21–22a)

But James has extended the analogy of murder from "sins of commission" only to "sins of omission" as well. *Not* to show mercy when mercy is demanded, he says, is to violate the law of Christ. And, along with that, to compound the unacceptable with a tendency to become obsequious and fawning towards the rich and powerful is to increase the oppression of the oppressed. It is soul-killing behavior, the antithesis of the "Law of freedom" and "the law of the kingdom."

Within the community of disciples, rigorous attention to maintaining equality and non-discrimination between its members is to be taken with utmost seriousness and regarded as indisputably mandatory. To observe that this has only been rarely the case in Christian history casts shame on that history.

2:14–26: The Divisive Doctrinal Issue: The Relationship of Faith and Works

¹⁴ Τί ὄφελος, ἀδελφοί μου, ἐὰν πίστιν λέγῃ τις ἔχειν ἔργα δὲ μὴ ἔχῃ; μὴ δύναται ἡ πίστις σῶσαι αὐτόν; ¹⁵ ἐὰν ἀδελφὸς ἢ ἀδελφὴ γυμνοὶ ὑπάρχωσιν καὶ λειπόμενοι τῆς ἐφημέρου τροφῆς, ¹⁶ εἴπῃ δέ τις αὐτοῖς ἐξ ὑμῶν· Ὑπάγετε ἐν εἰρήνῃ, θερμαίνεσθε καὶ χορτάζεσθε, μὴ δῶτε δὲ αὐτοῖς τὰ ἐπιτήδεια τοῦ σώματος, τί ὄφελος; ¹⁷ οὕτως καὶ ἡ πίστις, ἐὰν μὴ ἔχῃ ἔργα, νεκρά ἐστιν καθ᾽ ἑαυτήν. ¹⁸ Ἀλλ᾽ ἐρεῖ τις· Σὺ πίστιν ἔχεις κἀγὼ ἔργα ἔχω. δεῖξόν μοι τὴν πίστιν σου χωρὶς τῶν ἔργων, κἀγώ σοι δείξω ἐκ τῶν ἔργων μου τὴν πίστιν. ¹⁹ σὺ πιστεύεις ὅτι εἷς ἐστιν ὁ θεός; καλῶς ποιεῖς· καὶ τὰ δαιμόνια πιστεύουσιν καὶ φρίσσουσιν. ²⁰ θέλεις δὲ γνῶναι, ὦ ἄνθρωπε κενέ, ὅτι ἡ πίστις χωρὶς τῶν ἔργων ἀργή ἐστιν; ²¹ Ἀβραὰμ ὁ πατὴρ ἡμῶν οὐκ ἐξ ἔργων ἐδικαιώθη, ἀνενέγκας Ἰσαὰκ τὸν υἱὸν αὐτοῦ ἐπὶ τὸ θυσιαστήριον; ²² βλέπεις ὅτι ἡ πίστις συνήργει τοῖς ἔργοις αὐτοῦ καὶ ἐκ τῶν ἔργων ἡ πίστις ἐτελειώθη, ²³ καὶ ἐπληρώθη ἡ γραφὴ ἡ λέγουσα· Ἐπίστευσεν δὲ Ἀβραὰμ τῷ θεῷ, καὶ ἐλογίσθη αὐτῷ εἰς δικαιοσύνην, καὶ φίλος θεοῦ ἐκλήθη. ²⁴ ὁρᾶτε ὅτι ἐξ ἔργων δικαιοῦται ἄνθρωπος καὶ οὐκ ἐκ πίστεως μόνον. ²⁵ ὁμοίως δὲ καὶ Ῥαὰβ ἡ πόρνη οὐκ ἐξ ἔργων ἐδικαιώθη, ὑποδεξαμένη τοὺς ἀγγέλους καὶ ἑτέρᾳ ὁδῷ ἐκβαλοῦσα; ²⁶ ὥσπερ γὰρ τὸ σῶμα χωρὶς πνεύματος νεκρόν ἐστιν, οὕτως καὶ ἡ πίστις χωρὶς ἔργων νεκρά ἐστιν.

¹⁴*What is the profit, my brothers, if someone claims to have faith but does not have works? Is faith able to save him?* ¹⁵*If a brother or a sister are [sic] naked or lacking in daily food,* ¹⁶*And one of you says to them, "Go in peace, be warm and sated," but you do not give them the body's necessities, what is the profit?* ¹⁷*So also faith by itself, if it does not have works, is dead.* ¹⁸*Yet someone will say, "You have faith and I have works." You show me your faith without the works, and I will show you faith by my works.* ¹⁹*You have faith that God is one? You are doing well. Even the daemonic beings have that faith, and they tremble.* ²⁰*But are you willing to recognize, O you inane man, that faith without works yields nothing?* ²¹*Was not our father Abraham made righteous [or: proved righteous] by works, offering up his own son Isaac on the sacrificial altar?* ²²*You see that faith cooperated with his works, and by the works the faith was brought to completion,* ²³*And the scripture was fulfilled: "And Abraham had faith in God, and it was accounted to righteousness on his part," and he*

was called a friend of God. ²⁴*You see that a human being is made righteous [proved righteous] by works, and not by faith alone.* ²⁵*And, likewise, was not Rahab the prostitute also made righteous [proved righteous] by works, sheltering the messengers and sending them forth by a different path?* ²⁶*For just as the body without spirit [breath] is dead, so also faith without works is dead.*

It is unlikely, but not impossible, that James had in his possession copies of Paul's writings. But it is highly likely that reports about what Paul was teaching reached his ears, however garbled those reports may have been. Verses 14–26 are almost certainly to be read as a criticism of just such a garbled version of Paul's doctrine of "justification by faith" (a phrase that is better translated as "made righteous by faith" or "by faithfulness"), one which exaggerated that doctrine to infer that "faith" *alone*, irrespective of *moral* transformation, is sufficient for the follower of Christ—that is to say, that should one profess faith in the redemptive acts of Christ, one would be assured of being deemed "righteous" by God at the last judgment. How one conducted his or her life was thus theoretically of less importance than what one believed about Christ.

Paul himself had felt the need to condemn such a misconception of his views in his own letters. For example, to forestall any such false impression, he pointedly wrote to the Roman Christians: "What shall we say then? Should we persist in sin so that grace might abound? Let it not be! We who have died to sin, how shall we still live in it?" (Rom 6:1–2) And all his letters include lengthy passages of exhortations to live holy lives in conformity with the moral commandments of God. Whatever some of his hearers might have thought they heard him say, Paul himself never severed "justification by faith" from the requirement to fulfill "the Law's just ordinance" (Rom 8:4).

But Paul had also written such daring words as the following, words which might rather easily be misconstrued to imply that moral striving was not necessary for the believer (note my emphases in the examples that follow): "For we reckon a man as vindicated by faithfulness, *apart from* observances [or "works"] of Law" (Rom 3:28); "For if there is glory to *the ministry of condemnation* [i.e., the Law of Moses], the ministry of vindication [i.e., the gospel of Christ] abounds *much more* in glory" (2 Cor 3:9); "[We] who know that a human being is vindicated *not by observances of Law* but by the faithfulness of the Anointed One Jesus—even we have placed our faith in the Anointed One Jesus, so that we might be vindicated from the faithfulness of the Anointed and *not from observances of Law*, because *no flesh at all will be vindicated from observances of Law*" (Gal 2:16); and "*[For those who rely upon] observances of Law are under a curse*; for it has been written: 'Accursed is everyone who does not persevere in doing the things written in the book of the Law'" (Gal 3:10). Taken out of the larger context of his teaching, such sentiments as these could be misunderstood as saying that *faith*—meaning an intentional, sustained affirmation of what has been taught about Christ—stands in opposition to a mere law of *works* (or, as it is translated here, "observances"), and that one's "justification" or becoming "righteous" in the eyes of God has little or nothing to do with moral effort. Certainly, as we shall see, that was how James interpreted this doctrine, and it's why—we can suppose—he reacted as he did to correct it in his encyclical letter.

To add to the potential for confusion, Paul's teaching was complex, as his letters attest (one can sympathize with the pseudonymous author of 2 Peter, who wrote, decades after Paul's death, that the latter's writings are often "difficult to understand"; 2 Pet 3:16). Keeping up with Paul's rambling lines of reasoning or trying to make sense of all his convolutions and subtleties might well have taxed a number of his hearers, and no doubt they led to many misunderstandings. This is so much the case that even today his theology (and especially his soteriology) continues to be hotly debated. Some of Paul's teachings, in fact, remain open only to guesswork. That not all his contemporary hearers understood what he had said or written was a persistent state of affairs that Paul frequently endeavors to rectify in his epistles.

What appears to be the case, then, in the Letter of James is that a mangled version of Paul's gospel had come to James's notice. The key terms in their "debate" are *faith* and *works* (or "observances"), and the issue is whether or not the performing of *good works* is essential for being "righteous"—or "vindicated"—before God. In the corrupted version that James corrects in his letter, *both terms* had been misconstrued.

As we noted above, the real difference between James and Paul lay in how each of them valued *the Law*. Paul's view of the Law was ambivalent—it was basically "good," but it was also flawed (having been bestowed indirectly, which seems to be his meaning in Galatians 2:19: "[The Law was] ordained by angels in an intermediary's hand . . ."), and its role was to convict human beings of sin and make them aware that their condition was hopeless without the intervention of Christ.

James, however, unlike Paul, regarded the Law as positive and binding in its *moral* requirements. Even before the Letter of James was written, Paul's Letter to the Galatians had indicated that tensions existed between Paul and James. These *tensions*—we can't call them an open conflict—had flared up precisely over matters pertaining to how specific aspects of the Law were to be observed in the Christian community in Antioch, which numbered both Jews and gentiles among its members (see Gal 2:6, 11–12). There was, in other words, a "history" of friction between the two men. Given that history, which might already have made James at least partly wary of Paul, further news that a misconceived Pauline "gospel" was undermining moral principles laid down by Jesus (Matt 5:20) could have provoked James's rebuke in 2:14–26 above. Paul himself may have been, we can suppose, in prison at the time James wrote his epistle (cf. Acts 21:17—22:30). His letter, then, is not directed at Paul, who was effectively out of the way, but (as we have already noted) to communities that were indebted to Paul's ministry.

Although there were real differences, then, between James and Paul where the place of the Law in Christian life was concerned, what Paul had actually meant by *faith* and *works* was evidently not what James understood him to mean by those words.

Looking first at *faith*, the word can mean personal trust (a matter of "the heart," so to speak) or it can mean "belief" in the intellectual sense— say, a belief in a proposition or a doctrine. When *Paul* spoke of "faith" or "faithfulness," he had in mind the first meaning: a relationship based on personal *trust* (nor is it always clear whether Paul, in a number of passages in his writings, is referring to one's faith *in* Jesus, or to the faith *of* Jesus himself). Now, if James had understood that that was what Paul had meant by "faith"—a matter of "the heart"—there would likely have been no essential disagreement between the two. But it seems that what *James* had been given to understand was that by "faith" Paul had meant *belief* in the sense of *giving one's assent to a formal body of doctrine*—that is to say, "faith" was the mere acceptance of certain teachings (thus eliciting James's cutting jibe in verse 19: "You have faith [i.e., an intellectual belief] that God is one? You are doing well. Even the daemonic beings have that faith, and they tremble").

Similarly, by *works*, *Paul* had meant such outward customary "observances" prescribed in the Law as, for example, circumcision or the religious dietary regulations—in other words, *ceremonial* observances.

Again, if James had understood Paul's true meaning, one supposes that there would have been little disagreement between them. Following Jesus' example, many, if not most, Christian disciples—and gentile converts in particular—relegated ceremonial laws to be largely indifferent in character; such "works" as circumcision or ceremonial washings and the like were not considered essentials.

But what *James* meant by the very same term—"works"—were not ceremonial observances, but the essential *moral* obligations that are binding on disciples, especially those that relate to "the royal law" to love one's neighbor as oneself that we saw above in verse 8—for example, clothing the naked or feeding the hungry (vss. 15–16). For James, the *only* legitimate sign of authentic faith lies in *showing active love*—that is to say, *doing* "works" of visible charity, *doing good*. Jesus, after all, had taught his followers: "So let your light shine out before humanity, *so that they may see your good works and may glorify your Father in the heavens*" (Matt 5:16; emphasis mine.) And, again, we can suppose that Paul would not disagree—after all, in his same "tense" Letter to the Galatians, Paul had written that what "avails" in Christ is "faith *working* through love" (Gal 5:6, RSV; emphasis mine). Likewise, James might just as well have said in verse 26 in our passage above that "faith *without active love* is dead" as that "faith without works" is, and not have changed his basic point in the least.

So, the question must fairly be asked: is James mistakenly fighting empty concepts in these verses? Had he so misunderstood Paul's meaning that his own argument has no true relevance—either in his context or for later ages? I would suggest that, although James may have misunderstood what Paul meant by "faith" and "works," it was a misunderstanding that he apparently shared with a segment of *Paul's own followers*. His rebuke would therefore have been relevant at the time he wrote and, I believe, it has remained relevant ever since.

Is it not the case that, too often, Christians have substituted mere intellectual assent to a system of theological propositions in place of living trust or active "faithfulness"? Has it not frequently seemed that the affirmation of creedal orthodoxy is what matters most in the churches, while radical moral transformation and action, as Jesus taught, have been relegated to the status of respectable ideals (and often seen as being impractical in "the real world")? But, in fact, we get no support from the words of Jesus, Paul, or James—or from any text in the New Testament—that permits us to assume that "orthodoxy" trumps "orthopraxy," or that faith—rightly understood—can exist apart from works. And so it is that James's words in this passage should still cut its readers to the bone.

Verses 14–16 quite clearly spell out for us what James himself means by *works*: he means by that term *the active care of others in need*. Jesus had envisioned a community whose good and loving works were to be plainly visible before the world, so that God's kingdom or "empire" might be established on earth and that God might be seen in them. The earliest disciples, beginning in Jerusalem, endeavored to make this calling a reality (thus, for example, the mutual sharing of their goods and charity publicly exhibited to the destitute). So it was that James could not ignore the state of affairs in those churches he is most concerned to correct, in which this aspect of discipleship was being played down; they were not enacting, in other words, the dynamic of the genuine gospel of Jesus.

James refers to his hearers' "profit" and "salvation" in verse 14 ("What is the *profit*, my brothers, if someone claims to have faith but does not have works? Is faith able to *save* him?"). His pointed questions indicate that it is his readers' *actions* that should garner either praise or blame, not merely the conceptual content of their beliefs. If the world is to see the hope of salvation made manifest, it can only see it embodied in the actions of the disciple community. It is in their works where the truth and the life of their belief are seen to be real. And if the disciple community truly desires and proclaims salvation for others, it can only do this convincingly by enacting Christ's law of love before the watching eyes of the peoples among whom it dwells. James makes no bones about it—salvation *is* active love, and there will be no *profit* from one's faith unless that is *the* visible standard by which it lives.

Verses 17 and 26 stress this expectation by making the startling assertion that faith without works of love (i.e., the moral law) is *dead*. The verses that come between these two "bookend" verses flesh out the claim, but James gives us an image here that should linger in our minds. *Faith*, he says, is like a human body. It can be alive and well, or it can be sick and languishing (which might describe the spiritual state of those he addresses), or it can be completely dead and in the process of decaying. In the Law of Moses, a lifeless corpse was considered *unclean*, and so was anybody who came into contact with it or whatever it had touched:

> This is the law when a man dies in a tent: every one who comes
> into the tent, and every one who is in the tent, shall be unclean
> seven days . . . . Whoever in the open field touches one who is

slain with a sword, or a dead body, or a bone of a man, or a grave,
shall be unclean seven days . . . . And whatever the unclean person
touches shall be unclean; and anyone who touches it shall be unclean until evening. (Num 19:14–22)

James knows that his comparison of a lifeless "faith" (one without "spirit"
or "breath") to a lifeless body implies that the former is impure or unclean.
Again, we are reminded that he has already advocated *"pure and undefiled
religion"* (1:27), so his likening of a dead "faith" to an impure and contami-
nating corpse is particularly scathing. If faith is to be alive—that is to say, if
it is to be *real*—it must be vibrant with activity and health. It must *breathe*
and possess spirit. And the proof that it is in fact alive is that it *works*.

Verses 18 and 19, therefore, rebuke those who would divide faith and
works, putting asunder two aspects of what is essentially a single, indivisible
reality (and one cannot divide the breath from the body without death being the result). For James, faith *is* works and works *are the revealing of* faith.
Verse 18 is clumsily written, perhaps, but its meaning is obvious: real faith
can't exist apart from works. Works alone "show" faith's actuality. Verse 19,
then, ridicules a "faith" (that is to say, "belief" in the sense of acknowledg-
ing a conceptual truth—James cites as an example of this a merely intellectual assent to the Jewish formula that "God is one") that even demons
share. The sharpness of James's thrust is that one can be thoroughly evil and
yet possess a cerebral, but fruitless, "faith." And whatever demons may be,
apparently they are not theologically clueless, and so they have the good
sense to "tremble" before the reality they must begrudgingly confess. But
James implies that those who would presume to separate faith and works
haven't even the good sense demons possess. Just as "God is one," so faith
and works are one. To drive a wedge of abstract theory between them is an
aberration of the gospel, and to oppose one against the other is to disregard
the teachings of Christ.

In verses 20–25, James gives two examples of faith "cooperating"
(συνήργει—"synergy") with works in the accounts of Abraham "offering up
his own son Isaac" (Gen 22) and of "Rahab the prostitute" who "sheltered
the [Hebrew] messengers" (Josh 2:1–21; 6:17, 22–25).

The choice of Rahab as an illustration is a suggestive one, not because
she was a woman, but—more to the point—because she was a gentile.
James may be going out of his way here to include his gentile readers by
way of drawing on an instance of gentile heroism. Otherwise, Rahab could
be considered an odd choice and James's example somewhat strained,

equating as it does an act of deception on Rahab's part with the works of charity to the disadvantaged that James has been keen to stress above (1:27; 2:15–16). Rahab, of course, is also presented as an example (of faith, as it happens) in Hebrews 11:31, but in that chapter she is just one in a long list of worthies, and so she doesn't receive the same focused attention as James gives her. Here she is complementing the example of the patriarch, Abraham. In a similar vein, when we come to chapter five, we will see James holding up another gentile—in this case, Job—as an example to his readers of endurance (5:11), followed by the example of Elijah regarding prayerfulness (5:17). It is just possible, then, that James chose three non-Jews among his four exemplary biblical figures because he was sensitive to the fact that a significant number of his readers were themselves gentile converts.

Abraham, James's primary example, stands above the Jewish-gentile divide. He was the father of the Hebrew people, but a Chaldean himself. James's choice of Abraham as an example of "works" may be a pointed one, since he was used by Paul as an example of "faith apart from works" (Rom 4; Gal 3:6–29, 4:21–31). And, in fact, Paul quotes Genesis 15:6—"And Abraham had faith in God, and it was accounted to uprightness on his part"—just as James does above in verse 23. To simplify Paul's argument to its barest essentials, Abraham was "accounted righteous" before he was ever circumcised (one of the "works" of the Law that Paul regards as unnecessary for gentile believers), and it was his trust in God without such works that made him "righteous" in God's eyes. Thus, says Paul, following Abraham's example, gentiles do not need to be circumcised or submit to the Law's ceremonial observances ("works") in order to be liberated from slavery to sin and made righteous.

James's point, in contradistinction to Paul's, is that Abraham's saving "faith was brought to *completion*" through his "work" of obeying God in the matter of Isaac's "sacrifice." Again, as we have noted, by "works" James means the moral Law, not external observances such as circumcision. And as with his example of Rahab, the example of Abraham may also seem strained. After all, James's chief concern is really the essential place of loving works in Christian religion, but Abraham's willingness to offer up the life of his son could well appear to us to be anything but a loving work. And yet that supposition on our part would perhaps be to misunderstand the significance of this story within the larger tradition. Hebrews 11:17–19 reflects something of the importance "the binding of Isaac" had for early followers of Jesus, as well as for Judaism in general, emphasizing that it was a test of Abraham's *obedience* (and his faith, it should be noted, is said to have been so strong that he trusted that God could resurrect Isaac, even if the sacrifice had been completed). Similarly, James's emphasis is on *obedience* to what God and God's servant, Jesus the Anointed, commands. Abraham's initial faith could only be made evident by his subsequent willingness to *obey* God, which meant doing the difficult and painful thing he was commanded to do. The disciples' faith can likewise only be made evident by *obeying* the teachings of Christ—a commitment that is not always easy to maintain—to love, forgive, renounce all condemnation of others, perform good works for those in need, and so on.

Whether or not we find the "test" of Abraham's faith in Genesis 22 morally compelling in our day and age (and, understandably, we might find the analogy repellent), we should not lose sight of James's essential meaning: "You see that a human being is made righteous by works, and not by faith alone" (vs. 24). And "works" in James's mind refers not to any morally dubious demand for sacrifice like the one in his scriptural analogy, but to active obedience to the lovingly moral demands of Jesus. That, in turn, is nothing else than purified obedience to God's moral Law, which is what makes faith real, living, and attractive—a viable and visible alternative kingdom to the dominant kingdoms of "the cosmos." "So let your light shine out before men, so that they may see your good works and may glorify your Father in the heavens." (Matt 5:16)

3:1–12: Denunciation of Wrongful Use of the Tongue, With Focus on Those Who Would Teach Others

3.1 Μὴ πολλοὶ διδάσκαλοι γίνεσθε, ἀδελφοί μου, εἰδότες ὅτι μεῖζον κρίμα λημψόμεθα· 2 πολλὰ γὰρ πταίομεν ἅπαντες. εἴ τις ἐν λόγῳ οὐ πταίει, οὗτος τέλειος ἀνήρ, δυνατὸς χαλιναγωγῆσαι καὶ ὅλον τὸ σῶμα. 3 εἰ δὲ τῶν ἵππων τοὺς χαλινοὺς εἰς τὰ στόματα βάλλομεν εἰς τὸ πείθεσθαι αὐτοὺς ἡμῖν, καὶ ὅλον τὸ σῶμα αὐτῶν μετάγομεν. 4 ἰδοὺ καὶ τὰ πλοῖα, τηλικαῦτα ὄντα καὶ ὑπὸ ἀνέμων σκληρῶν ἐλαυνόμενα, μετάγεται ὑπὸ ἐλαχίστου πηδαλίου ὅπου ἡ ὁρμὴ τοῦ εὐθύνοντος βούλεται· 5 οὕτως καὶ ἡ γλῶσσα μικρὸν μέλος ἐστὶν καὶ μεγάλα αὐχεῖ. Ἰδοὺ ἡλίκον πῦρ ἡλίκην ὕλην ἀνάπτει· 6 καὶ ἡ γλῶσσα πῦρ, ὁ κόσμος τῆς ἀδικίας ἡ γλῶσσα καθίσταται ἐν τοῖς μέλεσιν ἡμῶν, ἡ σπιλοῦσα ὅλον τὸ σῶμα καὶ φλογίζουσα τὸν τροχὸν τῆς γενέσεως καὶ φλογιζομένη ὑπὸ τῆς γεέννης. ⁷πᾶσα γὰρ φύσις θηρίων τε καὶ πετεινῶν ἑρπετῶν τε καὶ ἐναλίων δαμάζεται καὶ δεδάμασται τῇ φύσει τῇ ἀνθρωπίνῃ· ⁸τὴν δὲ γλῶσσαν οὐδεὶς δαμάσαι δύναται ἀνθρώπων· ἀκατάστατον κακόν, μεστὴ ἰοῦ θανατηφόρου. ⁹ἐν αὐτῇ εὐλογοῦμεν τὸν κύριον καὶ πατέρα, καὶ ἐν αὐτῇ καταρώμεθα τοὺς ἀνθρώπους τοὺς καθ᾽ ὁμοίωσιν θεοῦ γεγονότας· ¹⁰ἐκ τοῦ αὐτοῦ στόματος ἐξέρχεται εὐλογία καὶ κατάρα. οὐ χρή, ἀδελφοί μου, ταῦτα οὕτως γίνεσθαι. ¹¹μήτι ἡ πηγὴ ἐκ τῆς αὐτῆς ὀπῆς βρύει τὸ γλυκὺ καὶ τὸ πικρόν; ¹²μὴ δύναται, ἀδελφοί μου, συκῆ ἐλαίας ποιῆσαι ἢ ἄμπελος σῦκα; οὔτε ἁλυκὸν γλυκὺ ποιῆσαι ὕδωρ.

¹*Not many of you should become teachers, brothers, as you know that we shall receive a greater judgment.* ²*For we all falter in numerous ways. If anyone does not falter in speech, he is a perfect man, able also to bridle his whole body.* ³*And, when we insert bridles into the mouths of horses to make them comply with us, we also direct their whole body.* ⁴*And look at how ships, which are so enormous and which are driven by powerful winds, are directed wherever the pilot's impulse determines by a tiny rudder;* ⁵*So also the tongue is a small bodily member, yet it boasts of great things. See how immense a forest so tiny a fire ignites.* ⁶*And the tongue is a fire, iniquity's cosmos, defiling the whole body, and setting aflame the wheel of generation, and being itself set aflame by Hinnom's Vale.* ⁷*For every nature—both of beasts and of birds, both of reptiles and of creatures of the sea—is being tamed, and has been tamed, by human nature,* ⁸*But from among human beings there is no one able to tame the tongue: a restless evil full of lethal venom.* ⁹*With it we bless the Lord and Father, and with it we curse human beings who have been born according to God's likeness;* ¹⁰*Out of the same mouth comes blessing and curse. It is not fitting, my brothers, that these things happen thus.* ¹¹*Does the fountain issue forth from the same spout as both sweet and bitter?* ¹²*Can a fig tree produce olives, my brothers, or a vine figs? Neither can what is salty produce sweet water.*

It could be tempting to read James's epistle as—at least in part—a response to Paul's Letter to the Galatians, so close does James seem in places almost to be making a rebuttal to that letter's main theme and, to be blunt, even to its excesses. However, to attempt to make a case that James had Paul's most angry letter in mind when he wrote his would be to push matters much too far. I will suggest, however, that it may be no coincidence that James immediately follows up his contradiction of the misconstrued Pauline doctrine regarding faith and works in the last passage with a sharp warning here that not "many" should assume the mantle of "teachers" *unless* they have learned to restrain their tongues (vs. 1). Specifically, James is remonstrating with "teachers" who too freely use their tongues even to the point of pronouncing *curses* on others (vs. 9). Teachers, he says, including himself, "shall receive greater judgment" than the rest. This is because, presumably, they are taking upon themselves the task of being guides and examples. Clearly, this entire passage is making the argument that one cannot both be a conduit of blessing (as a teacher of Christ's good news should be) and a conduit of condemnation (God, after all, being entirely perfect in his love, according to James—the source of "every good act of giving" and the one "with whom there is no alternation or shadow of change"; 1:17).

Having, then, dealt with an aberrant version of Pauline teaching that seemed to discount the moral Law, James may very well be addressing in these verses those who have adopted an unfortunate personal characteristic of Paul's—one that was having negative consequences for the maintenance of concord among the communities.

I think we have every reason to assume that, if Paul was capable of expressing himself by letter as he did with the Galatians, he could—and probably did—express himself in similar fashion in person and in other non-extant writings. What we have as proof of this tendency—Exhibit A, if you will—is his Letter to the Galatians. In that epistle Paul communicates his anger at what he saw as an intrusion into his churches by those preaching "a different gospel"—a "gospel" that stipulated that gentile believers should be circumcised and keep the Law in all its ceremonial particulars. With that insistence Paul quite justifiably took issue. Although we can sympathize with his frustration and even his outbursts to the Galatian communities, he nevertheless waxes intemperate even to the point of crudity: "Would that they who are causing you agitation might just castrate themselves!" (Gal 5:12) No doubt, it might be easy for some to read that bawdy turn of phrase with amusement, but Paul was not trying to amuse. His exasperation is volatile and all too visible. Worse than that, he pronounces a curse (although he tempers it rhetorically with the mention of "we or an angel out of heaven"): "But, even if we or an angel out of heaven should proclaim [to you] good tidings that differ from what you received, let him be accursed [ἀνάθεμα]. As I have just said, and now say again, if anyone proclaims good tidings to you differing from what you received, let him be accursed [ἀνάθεμα]." (Gal. 1:8–9) Assuming that Paul had a propensity for intemperate rhetoric—something his letters indicate rather strongly—we can, and probably should, imagine that his most ardent imitators could have seen in his example license to exhibit similar conduct when opportunities for zealousness arose, condemning harshly any suspected of proclaiming a "different gospel" and calling down the occasional ἀνάθεμα (anathema) if "righteously" stirred up to do so.

Psychologically, this is not uncommon behavior on the part of followers of someone who is especially admired. An influential person exudes charisma—and Paul certainly did, despite his tendency to self-effacement—and even his or her flaws take on a certain appeal for his or her admirers. Those who view such a person as a model for their own lives and personal formation may adopt not only their ideas but also their mannerisms. If that same influential person had allowed himself to indulge in certain unfortunate freedoms of expression or behavior, his followers might well follow suit and take on those same tendencies, lacking the critical faculty needed to discern what was truly admirable in that individual from what was not, and even exaggerating and almost sanctifying his worst tendencies.

And, unfortunately, immature imitations can also, over time, harden into normative styles and methodologies. Take the idea of "anathematizing"—cursing—those for whom one feels a supposedly "righteous," perhaps even defensible, indignation. Paul, in a blaze of anger, anathematizes those who have agitated the Galatian communities, condemning their "gospel" and them along with it. One can easily imagine Paul's imitators in turn doing precisely the same with those with whom they might disagree later. And, indeed, during the centuries that followed, the tendency to anathematize "heretics" became what we should today be able to acknowledge for what it was—a disgraceful scandal. Even before the age of Constantine, we know that there were numerous instances of Christians, orthodox and heretical both, attacking physically and even killing one another over such issues as the "proper" understanding of "the two natures" of Christ. In 385, the empire having by that time become fully "Christianized" under the emperor Theodosius, the first "heretics" were *executed*—having first, of course, been officially anathematized by the church. So prevalent the tendency to condemn "false teachers" became that every ecumenical council of the church concluded its sessions with a string of anathemas. That none of this can be defended by recourse to Jesus should be self-evident. Nor can we hold Paul accountable for the multitude of anathemas—compounded by official inquisitions and judicial killings—that mar the church's history, east and west. One can be sure that such misery and viciousness would have sickened the great apostle who had also written so movingly of love.

But, it seems, James already sensed something of the potential harm that, in seminal form, may have existed in the intemperate speech of Paul's imitators and even of Paul himself, great though the latter unquestionably was.

If we allow our imagination some free rein here, we might picture the position in which James found himself. We can surmise, from what evidence exists, that he was the one who stood somewhere between Paul and those whom Paul opposed in Galatia and elsewhere. James may very well have felt a duty to both sides in the dispute so as to hold the fledgling churches together.

Paul is careful in Galatians not to impugn James directly, but his waspish references to James in that letter are intended, it would appear, to bring him down a peg or two. James is most likely included among those esteemed worthies in the Jerusalem church from whom Paul snappishly says he had received nothing of worth: "And from those who were esteemed as something—precisely what sort of something at that time does not matter to me (God does not take a man at his face)—for to me these estimable men had nothing to add . . . ." (Gal 2:6; see Gal 1:18–19) And in Galatians 2:12 we find that those who had unsettled relations between Jewish and gentile believers in the church at Antioch had come "along with James." Paul's specific allusion to James's emissaries in Antioch, as those responsible for stirring up discord there, seems to insinuate that his later troubles in the Galatian churches were—at least in Paul's mind—somehow also connected with James's people. But, again, Paul seems careful not to impugn James himself. What all this may indicate is that James was, as he is depicted in the gathering described in Acts 15, the arbiter or mediator between two extremes: on the one hand, those seeking greater adherence to Jewish observances, even for gentiles, and, on the other, Paul and his followers, who saw such attempts to enforce the Law as a form of "enslaving" those who should be "free" from it (Gal 2:4). James may have possessed the coolest head of the lot, regarding both extremes as problematic—the legalists for their overstepping and demanding too much, and Paul for his quick-tempered and seemingly unreasonable reaction to them. For James, it would appear that the most important quality to cling to in any dispute between brethren was the self-restraint necessary for muffling recriminations and controlling the tongue. In this, he elevates Jesus' teaching that speech and gracious conduct should be paramount in our dealings—even, presumably, over perplexing matters of doctrine.

This brings us back to the passage above. We can certainly read James 3:1–12 as a general pastoral exhortation against sins of the tongue. Its lessons are applicable on that level, applicable to everyone. Neither are we compelled to adopt the sort of hypothetical background that I've proposed above to give a context to these verses. On the other hand, I believe there is enough internal evidence—both in the Letter of James and in Paul's Letter to the Galatians, as well as in the book of Acts—to buttress my conjectures. Either way, James never mentions Paul by name. It could be that he didn't have Paul (or even his followers) in mind in this passage after all, although I would rather be inclined to believe that James's reticence to name names speaks more of his composure and self-restraint. He doesn't condemn or judge *persons*, but does rebuke *behavior*—as, in fact, Jesus had taught his disciples to do. And, more to the point, in 3:1–12 he is specifically warning those who are calling themselves *teachers*. To understand this passage rightly, then, we need to recognize that he is explicitly rebuking those who presume to teach in Christ's name while at the same time *cursing* others. That, in a nutshell, is his main point.

There is little need to explain the passage. Its language is straightforward and pastoral. Verses 2–5 stress how the tongue is the one member of the body most difficult to contain. By saying that "we all falter in numerous ways" and that "if anyone does not falter in speech, he is a perfect man" (vs. 2), James is showing himself sympathetic to, but not making excuses for, such failure. Quite the opposite, he means to say that controlling the tongue requires earnest effort—and those who make no effort to do that should not be overly eager to teach. To make disciples, one must teach by example as much as by words.

James's string of metaphors is forceful and intended to convict the overconfident. Perhaps the most striking metaphor he uses is that of the fire of "Hinnom's Vale" (γέεννα) or, as it is usually transliterated, "gehenna" (the old usage of the word "hell" is a singularly unfortunate and wildly inaccurate rendering). James is, in fact, the only epistolary writer in the New Testament who uses the term—all the other references to it appearing in the Synoptic Gospels, and in Matthew almost twice as many times as in the other two Gospels combined (Matthew uses it seven times, Mark three, and Luke just once). It is noteworthy that James uses an image so familiar to us from Jesus' own lexicon, underscoring again the closeness of their conceptual views. To say that the abusive tongue is "set aflame by Hinnom's Vale" is a difficult—maybe impossible—image to elucidate adequately (once we set aside, as we ought, the customary mental pictures we have of an underworld "hell"), but possibly it may suggest yet another hint of the uncleanness associated with death. Certainly the picture we have of gehenna from Jesus' sayings—"where their worm does not die and their fire is not quenched" (Mark 9:48)—derives from the scene of the aftermath of slaughter in Isaiah 66:24: "And they shall go forth and look on the dead bodies of the men that have rebelled against me; for their worm shall not die, their fire shall not be quenched, and they shall be an abhorrence to all flesh." However we understand the image as James employs it, there is an unmistakable stench of judgment, decay, and death about it—and James means his readers to understand that this is the "spiritual" condition of the abusive tongue.

He reaches a culmination with these devastating words: "With [the tongue] we bless the Lord and Father, and with it we curse human beings who have been born according to God's likeness; out of the same mouth comes blessing and curse. It is not fitting, my brothers, that these things happen thus." (Vss. 9–10) We should note in passing, that verse 12 ("Can a fig tree produce olives, my brothers, or a vine figs?") echoes Jesus' words of warning against "false prophets" in Matthew 7:16 ("Persons do not gather grapes from thorns or figs from thistles, do they?").

James's message in this passage, rooted in the teachings of Jesus before him, remains as timelessly important as ever. It is also applicable in these days to those in positions of pastoral influence who write books or blogs, who engage others on social media or websites, who produce podcasts or seek to guide others in numerous other venues. If one adopts the role of teacher, he or she is obligated to restrain what one says—either in speech or on the keyboard. There should be no condemning of others' persons, no personal denunciations disguised as "heresy hunting," no self-righteous nitpicking, no spreading of scurrilous stories, and no "official" anathemas. We should note James's *reticence* as exemplary—he excoriates bad behavior and poor example, but not specific persons.

We should also bear in mind how James, following Jesus, depicts the nature of God—he is perfect, unchangingly good, the giver of wisdom, in whom exists no dark shadow. He is the only lawgiver and judge. Those who speak in his name have no license to despise, denounce, or curse others, seeing that such behavior flagrantly misrepresents God and his Anointed. Indeed, as the verses that follow (3:13–18) confirm, James's conviction is that what should denote the character of the disciple and the teacher of disciples alike is *divine wisdom*, which he describes as "pure, then peaceable, reasonable, accommodating, full of mercy and good fruits, impartial, unfeigned" (3:17)—in short, characteristics wholly at odds with the very characteristics he has just censured.

And this brings us directly to the theme of friendship with God, who is the source of divine wisdom:

3:13—4:10: What is Required for Friendship with God

Those whom James has called "divided in soul" (or "two-souled") in 1:8 are brought up again in 4:8 below. It's a significant designation, revealing that there is an inner conflict at work that needs to be resolved among those he addresses. They are torn between God and "the cosmos" and thus between divine wisdom and a false "wisdom." Although he doesn't use the term directly, James is issuing a call to repentance—μετάνοια (*metanoia*)—a word that literally means a change of one's thoughts or mind. Those professing allegiance to God and his Anointed are therefore exhorted to draw near to God and to leave behind entirely the ways of "the Slanderer" or "the devil" (ὁ διάβολος; 4:7). Above all, this portion is a call for those in the communities he is addressing to "make peace" with one another (3:18). Without such peace between the followers of Jesus, true friendship with God is not possible.

James's call resounds with the sort of language so often employed by the Old Testament prophets. Given the force and fervor of his words, we can—once again—only assume that he is addressing an *actual conflict* that has arisen among the churches. He isn't adopting mere rhetorical flourish for effect, or writing a general appeal for edification's sake. Something genuinely harmful to the community of disciples is being confronted here, something so threatening that it entails using such harsh terms as "adulteresses" and "enemy of God" (4:4) to warn those most in need of repentance. We cannot know the context, although we can suppose it is directly related to the doctrinal dispute regarding faith and works we have discussed above. To repeat a key theme of this commentary, this entire epistle is far more cohesive than is occasionally proposed, and we can assume that all its exhortations are linked together as one overall concern. We can also be certain that the situation James is addressing is one of severe communal discord, possibly of churches in the process of fracturing.

f. *Two Kinds of Wisdom (3:13–18)*

¹³ Τίς σοφὸς καὶ ἐπιστήμων ἐν ὑμῖν; δειξάτω ἐκ τῆς καλῆς ἀναστροφῆς τὰ ἔργα αὐτοῦ ἐν πραΰτητι σοφίας. ¹⁴ εἰ δὲ ζῆλον πικρὸν ἔχετε καὶ ἐριθείαν ἐν τῇ καρδίᾳ ὑμῶν, μὴ κατακαυχᾶσθε καὶ ψεύδεσθε κατὰ τῆς ἀληθείας. ¹⁵ οὐκ ἔστιν αὕτη ἡ σοφία ἄνωθεν κατερχομένη, ἀλλὰ ἐπίγειος, ψυχική, δαιμονιώδης· ¹⁶ ὅπου γὰρ ζῆλος καὶ ἐριθεία, ἐκεῖ ἀκαταστασία καὶ πᾶν φαῦλον πρᾶγμα. ¹⁷ ἡ δὲ ἄνωθεν σοφία πρῶτον μὲν ἁγνή ἐστιν, ἔπειτα εἰρηνική, ἐπιεικής, εὐπειθής, μεστὴ ἐλέους καὶ καρπῶν ἀγαθῶν, ἀδιάκριτος, ἀνυπόκριτος· ¹⁸ καρπὸς δὲ δικαιοσύνης ἐν εἰρήνῃ σπείρεται τοῖς ποιοῦσιν εἰρήνην.

¹³*Who among you is wise and knowledgeable? Let him display his works by comely conduct in wisdom's gentleness.* ¹⁴*But, if you harbor bitter jealousy and selfish ambition in your heart, do not boast and speak falsely against the truth.* ¹⁵*This is not the wisdom that descends from above, but is earthly, natural, daemoniacal;* ¹⁶*For where there are jealousy and selfish ambition, there is disorder and every squalid deed.* ¹⁷*But the wisdom from above is first of all pure, then peaceable, reasonable, accommodating, full of mercy and good fruits, impartial, unfeigned.* ¹⁸*And the fruit of righteousness is sown in peace for those who make peace.*

James in these verses, we may take for granted, continues to address those who would have themselves deemed "teachers" (3:1), in other words, those who wish to be known as "wise and knowledgeable" (vs. 13). Jews counted on their rabbis and elders to be such. James is therefore traditional in his expectation that a teacher must "display his works by comely conduct in wisdom's gentleness" (vs. 13). Note that the emphasis is again on "his *works*" (τὰ ἔργα αὐτοῦ), which James says are made visible only "in . . . gentleness" (ἐν πραΰτητι)—the word πραΰτης meaning, among other things, to be *humble* and *unpretentious*. The characteristics of divinely bestowed wisdom listed in verse 17 ("pure," "peaceable," "reasonable" or "considerate," "accommodating," "full of mercy and good fruits," "impartial" or not being overly critical, and "unfeigned") are all attributes of unpretentiousness, humility, and "gentleness." James is demanding that *peace* should reign in the communities he is exhorting—which he makes explicit in verse 18: "And the fruit of righteousness is sown in *peace* for those who make *peace*"—and peace within the communities can only be established if those tasked with teaching and pastoral oversight exercise exemplary reasonableness, coolheadedness, kindness, and gentleness of conduct themselves.

Verses 14–16, then, provide us with a portrait of the sort of posturing that James is rebuking. He lists in these verses counter-attributes of the wise gentleness he demands: the infection of "bitter jealousy" or "bitter zealotry" or "bitter opinionatedness"—which we can understand to mean a combative, unyielding, argumentative, and discordant character; a person given to unreasonable extremes, regardless of the disharmony it produces. Likewise, he censures "selfish ambition," which can mean here something like an "overbearing" personality whose influence succeeds in dividing people into "parties."

James implies that there is another sort of "wisdom" at work here, not that he directly calls it "wisdom." He refers to this false but—in the eyes of some—*seeming* wisdom as "earthly," "natural" or merely "animal" (ψυχική), and "daemoniacal" (δαιμονιώδης)—which could perhaps be translated, with some justification, as "diabolical" (vs. 15). With the last of those three designations—"daemoniacal"—we are reminded of the "unclean spirits" or "unclean breaths" that were believed could take up residence in a person and influence his or her thoughts and actions. We see this belief illustrated in the accounts of Jesus' casting out of "evil spirits" or "demons" in the Gospels. To be under the influence of an evil spirit is a condition considered antithetical to being occupied by God's Spirit, and that is probably James's assumption here.

To conclude with this passage, a teacher with personal influence or natural charisma has the capacity to come across to others as eminently wise, and yet he may be the very antithesis of divine wisdom. Such a teacher is "known by his fruits" (cf. Matt 7:16): "For where there are jealousy and selfish ambition, there is disorder and every squalid deed" (vs. 16). In other words, the community is divided and people are venomously set at odds with one another, defending their factions and preferred interpretations of doctrine. Meanwhile the genuine teachings of Jesus regarding the essentials of love, forgiveness, and mercy are undermined by doctrinaire extremism, rivalry, and bitter zeal.

g. *Either Friendship with "the Cosmos" or Friendship with God, But Not with Both (4:1–10)*

4:1 Πόθεν πόλεμοι καὶ πόθεν μάχαι ἐν ὑμῖν; οὐκ ἐντεῦθεν, ἐκ τῶν ἡδονῶν ὑμῶν τῶν στρατευομένων ἐν τοῖς μέλεσιν ὑμῶν; ² ἐπιθυμεῖτε, καὶ οὐκ ἔχετε· φονεύετε καὶ ζηλοῦτε, καὶ οὐ δύνασθε ἐπιτυχεῖν· μάχεσθε καὶ πολεμεῖτε. οὐκ ἔχετε διὰ τὸ μὴ αἰτεῖσθαι ὑμᾶς. ³ αἰτεῖτε καὶ οὐ λαμβάνετε, διότι κακῶς αἰτεῖσθε, ἵνα ἐν ταῖς ἡδοναῖς ὑμῶν δαπανήσητε. ⁴ μοιχαλίδες, οὐκ οἴδατε ὅτι ἡ φιλία τοῦ κόσμου ἔχθρα τοῦ θεοῦ ἐστιν; ὃς ἐὰν οὖν βουληθῇ φίλος εἶναι τοῦ κόσμου, ἐχθρὸς τοῦ θεοῦ καθίσταται. ⁵ ἢ δοκεῖτε ὅτι κενῶς ἡ γραφὴ λέγει· Πρὸς φθόνον ἐπιποθεῖ τὸ πνεῦμα ὃ κατῴκισεν ἐν ἡμῖν; ⁶ μείζονα δὲ δίδωσιν χάριν· διὸ λέγει· Ὁ θεὸς ὑπερηφάνοις ἀντιτάσσεται ταπεινοῖς δὲ δίδωσιν χάριν. ⁷ ὑποτάγητε οὖν τῷ θεῷ· ἀντίστητε δὲ τῷ διαβόλῳ, καὶ φεύξεται ἀφ᾽ ὑμῶν· ⁸ ἐγγίσατε τῷ θεῷ, καὶ ἐγγιεῖ ὑμῖν. καθαρίσατε χεῖρας, ἁμαρτωλοί, καὶ ἁγνίσατε καρδίας, δίψυχοι. ⁹ ταλαιπωρήσατε καὶ πενθήσατε καὶ κλαύσατε· ὁ γέλως ὑμῶν εἰς πένθος μετατραπήτω καὶ ἡ χαρὰ εἰς κατήφειαν. ¹⁰ ταπεινώθητε ἐνώπιον κυρίου, καὶ ὑψώσει ὑμᾶς.

4:1 *Where do the conflicts and where do the battles among you come from? Is it not from there—from the pleasures waging war in your bodily members?* ² *You desire and you do not have; you murder and covet and you are unable to obtain; you fight and wage war; you do not have because you do not ask;* ³ *You ask and do not receive because you ask in an evil fashion, so that you might spend on your own pleasures.* ⁴ *You adulteresses, do you not know that friendship with the cosmos is enmity with God? Whoever therefore resolves to be a friend of the cosmos is rendered an enemy of God.* ⁵ *Or do you think it in vain that the scripture says, "The spirit that has dwelt within us yearns to the point of envy?" [6]But he gives greater grace. Hence it says, "God opposes the arrogant but gives grace to the humble." [7]Therefore, be subordinate to God, but oppose the Slanderer and he will flee from you. [8]Draw near to God and he will draw near to you. Cleanse your hands, you sinners, and purify your hearts, you double-souled men. [9]Be distressed and mourn and weep; let your laughter be turned to mourning and your joy to dejection. [10]Be humbled before the Lord and he will lift you up.*

The first Christian community, the one that James would eventually preside over, is portrayed in Acts 4:32 as the prototype for all the churches: "And both the heart and the soul of the multitude of those who had come to have faith were one, and no one said that any of the possessions belonging to him was his own, but everything was owned among them communally." Two features are emphasized in this verse, with the second feature being an expression of the first: (1) the community was so united in spirit that they could be said to be "one", and (2) this was seen in the common sharing of their material goods. Luke writes that "both the *heart* and the *soul*" of the church's members—terms indicating their spiritual bond and mutual love—were such that communal distribution was the complementary result. Another way to put it is that their faith made them *selfless* in their conduct towards one another. If Luke depicts that original Christian community somewhat accurately—and there is no convincing reason to doubt that he does, even if it is an idealized picture—then, as we commented earlier, we can suppose that it served as the model for James's idea of Christian community throughout his life.

What we find James decrying in 4:1–10 is the antithesis of that model. As indicated above, James's circular epistle is addressing actual splits in the churches. As we note in other New Testament letters (e.g., 1 and 2 Corinthians, Galatians, 2 Peter, Jude, the Johannine epistles), conflicts in the church became widespread within the earliest decades. James suggests in these verses just how intense the storms and strife could be, not hesitating to use words like "conflicts," "battles," "war," and "murder." These terms are not to be taken literally, of course, but as trenchant metaphors (by the fourth century, sadly, they could very well have been understood literally). Christians were not (yet) shedding each other's blood, but—as James knew—it is only a matter of degree between hatred and murder. Jesus had indicated as much in his teaching: "You have heard that it was said to those of ancient times: 'You shall not commit murder; and whoever commits murder shall be liable to judgment.' Whereas I say to you that everyone who becomes angry with his brother shall be liable to judgment . . . ." (Matt 5:21–22) We find a similar, though blunter, sentiment in 1 John 3:15: "Everyone who hates his brother is a murderer, and you know that no murderer has the life of the Age abiding in him."

James traces these communal conflicts to their roots, the latter being inner and spiritual in nature. If the ideal of unity of heart and soul, as seen in Acts 4:32, is an inner one that works outwards from *selflessness* to *sharing*, what James is witnessing in those he exhorts is an inner "war" that begins in *selfishness* and ends in *fighting*.

The word "pleasures" in verse 1 (ἡδονῶν) reveals what occupies the "hearts and souls" of those he reprimands. As he has already castigated wealthy believers above, and will again below, we can suppose that it is most likely those with means whose "pleasures" (along with a doctrine of work-less faith) receive this sharp rebuke. These unspecified "pleasures" are rooted, he says, in their "bodily members," where they are said to be "waging war" with (one assumes) "the spirit that has dwelt within us" (vs. 5).

James (like Paul and other New Testament writers) views each man and woman as undergoing an inner struggle between the "body" (or, in Paul's favored term, "the flesh") and the "spirit." Our "bodily members" pull us towards self-centered "pleasures" (and are also bound to death, because bodies die), while our "spirit" (πνεῦμα) draws us towards God: "Or do you think it in vain that the scripture says, 'The spirit that has dwelt within us yearns to the point of envy?'" (vs. 5). It isn't clear what "scripture" James has in mind here, although Exodus 20:5 and Wisdom 6:23 have been suggested; or—more likely in my estimation—he may be quoting a text that no longer survives. Nor is it certain that "spirit" in this case means "God's Spirit," although that seems to be the best guess. The verse is notoriously obscure and difficult to translate with any assurance of absolute accuracy. But, with that admitted, we can understand the gist, which we might elucidate somewhat by citing a parallel verse from Paul's Letter to the Galatians (!): "For the flesh longs in opposition to the spirit, and the spirit in opposition to the flesh, inasmuch as they are opposed one to the other, so that you might not do as you would wish." (Gal 5:17) James's understanding of the body/flesh and spirit is essentially the same as Paul's: each person contains within himself or herself a conflict of interests, a tug of war. What can transcend that interior, individual conflict, though, is communal solidarity, through which each member receives help from, and is sustained by, all the other members of the community. And in that sort of common life one moves away from *selfish pleasure-seeking* to *selfless love*—with all the benefits that that provides.

Verses 2–3 describe the sort of communal life that results when individual self-seeking becomes the behavioral standard: "You [plural throughout] desire and you do not have; you murder and covet and you are unable to obtain; you fight and wage war; you do not have because you do not ask; you ask and do not receive because you ask in an evil fashion, so that you might spend on your own pleasures." In other words, things degenerate in every area of the community's existence. Internally, each one is frustrated in one's "desire" (ἐπιθυμεῖτε—a term which usually has a negative connotation), gives in to hatred of others ("murder" is the apt metaphor), and is covetous of others' goods and gifts. On the other hand, prayers are either neglected or performed selfishly ("in an evil fashion") with each one's eyes fastened on the attainment of one's "own pleasures." This not only makes for miserable persons, but for the dissolution of community.

At this point, I will venture to suggest that James traces a direct line from that misconstrued "gospel" of "faith alone" that we saw in chapter two, which denies the essentiality of works, to the sort of infectious selfishness and communal conflict he condemns here. The text is unbroken and presumably so is the moral logic of it. In other words, chapters two through four are essentially linked together. In them we find both cause and effects.

James echoes the language of the Old Testament prophets in the verses that follow. Referring to those he calls "double-souled" (vs. 8; see 1:8) as "adulteresses" (vs. 4) reminds us that the covenantal union between God and his people is often described in nuptial terms in the Scriptures, the betrayal of which covenant, by worshiping false gods, is considered "adultery" (cf., for example, Isa 54:5ff; Jer 2:1ff; Ezek 16; Hos 2 and 3).

In this case, though, the "false god" to beware consorting with here is "the cosmos" itself—which is usually translated as "the world." "Cosmos," which is not a translation but a transliteration, includes much more in scope than our word "world" implies in our own day, reduced as the latter is to indicating only the strictly tangible. In the purview of "the cosmos" are things visible and invisible, things of this earth and also beyond it, things we can comprehend and things beyond human ken. The warning in verse 7 to "oppose the Slanderer" (*diabolo* = "devil") reminds us that, first, what the devil does is *slander* ("defame" and "vilify")—a title that implies a relation to the sins of the tongue denounced in chapter three. Second, it reminds us that the cosmos includes such a malign presence and activity. This is a common New Testament trope. We find something very similar, for instance, in 1 John 5:19: "We know that we are of God, and that the whole cosmos rests entirely upon the wicked one." If there is a conflict between body and spirit, then, there is also one between "the cosmos" and God.

Here we must be careful not to carry this idea too far, as some did in those churches that were eventually lured into a heterodox "gnostic" view of reality (although early orthodox writers also saw themselves as "gnostics," or those possessing "knowledge" of the truth), a view that confused "the cosmos" with the whole of creation and thereby tended to reject both as essentially flawed. For James and the other New Testament writers, "the cosmos" does not simply mean "the earth" or "creation" or anything that is deemed essentially good. The "cosmos" in New Testament thought is something of an unwholesome overlay, "spiritual" in origin, though with human collusion, corrupting in its influence, and which ultimately must undergo judgment and dissolution ("And the cosmos is passing away, as well as its desire, but whoever does the Father's will abides unto the Age"; 1 John 2:17). In classical Christian terms, "the cosmos" is the dominion of sin and death, from which the creation must be purged. What will emerge from that critical purgation will be a restored creation, cleansed of all devilish and human-made defilement—cleansed, that is, of what distinguishes "the cosmos" from the creation as God intended it. This transformation has already begun in the coming of the Anointed One, through his sacrificial death (taking away sin) and empowering resurrection (overcoming death).

If we understand this perspective—that one *cannot* be wedded to, or be an intimate friend with, "the cosmos," which must ultimately disappear, and not risk disappearing along with it by so doing—then James's warnings become clearer and strike us as more urgent than ever. One is either a "friend" of the passing cosmos or a "friend" of God; in other words, either one perishes with this age or lives now and in the Age to come. James's stress on wisdom in his epistle and on friendship with God are reminiscent of the tradition we find in the book of Wisdom, that God's wisdom makes us God's friends (Wis 7:27–28).

Verses 6–10, then, constitute a call for these communities to humble themselves, to repent, and to mourn their infidelity. Verse 6 quotes Proverbs 3:34. The charge in verse 8 to "cleanse the hands" and "purify the heart"—so that those he reprimands will be *single* in their focus and goals, as opposed to being "*double*-souled" or duplicitous—echoes the words of Psalm 24:4–5: "He who has clean hands and a pure heart, who does not lift up his soul to what is false, and does not swear deceitfully . . . will receive blessing from the Lord, and vindication from the God of his salvation." And verses 9–10 ("Be distressed and mourn and weep; let your laughter be turned to mourning and your joy to dejection. Be humbled before the Lord and he will lift you up") are not to be understood as a summons to a perpetual state of mind, but to *a communal act of confession of sin*, mutual forgiveness, and renewal of commitment to God. We should place the emphasis in verse 10 on the promise that, in response to such self-humbling, God "will lift you up." And, likewise, in verse 6, the stress should be on the assurance that God "gives greater grace" in the struggle between the bodily members and the Spirit to those willing to exercise humility. These verses are, in fact, a restatement of the prophet Micah's words of grace: "He has showed you, O man, what is good; and what does the LORD require of you but to do justice, and to love kindness, and to walk humbly with your God?" (Mic 6:8) They also put us in mind of Isaiah 58, with its summons to communal humility through what is designated by the prophet as the "true fast" God desires—which is, significantly, a self-sacrificing discipline for the renewal of the people's care for the poor and the oppressed and the curbing of wicked speech:

> Is not this the fast that I choose: to loose the bonds of wickedness, to undo the thongs of the yoke, to let the oppressed go free, and to break every yoke? Is it not to share your bread with the hungry, and bring the homeless poor into your house; when you see the naked, to cover him, and not to hide yourself from your own flesh? Then shall your light break forth like the dawn, and your healing shall spring up speedily; your righteousness shall go before you, the glory of the LORD shall be your rear guard. Then you shall call, and the LORD will answer; you shall cry, and he will say, Here I am. If you take away from the midst of you the yoke, the pointing of the finger, and speaking wickedness, if you pour yourself out for the hungry and satisfy the desire of the afflicted, then shall your light rise in the darkness and your gloom be as the noonday. (Isa 58:6–10)

Lastly, it is significant to note that, although James sees conflict on the macrocosmic level ("the cosmos" opposed to God) and on the microcosmic level (the "bodily members" opposed to the "spirit" in each individual), his supreme hope is that perfect union will be realized. The temporal cosmos is not in any real sense in competition with the everlasting God. It is not to be simply identified with God's creation, as we have said, but is rather a sort of intrusive overlay on the creation—like a window which has become begrimed, obscuring the sunlight. It isn't coextensive with creation, and its time is limited. One who "befriends" it or "weds" what is only temporary, therefore, will be bereft when its time has passed. To "draw near to God" (vs. 8), therefore, means to be purified of "double-souledness," with its half-hearted attachment to the ephemeral, and thereby to establish a completely inseparable union of will with the everlasting God. For James, *the great problem is conflict and disharmony* (macrocosmic and microcosmic), and *the solution is union* between God and his creation and God and the human being. Those who single-mindedly pursue such a harmony must by necessity also strive to be at peace with one another.

For the ever-pragmatic James, communal unity is not primarily a matter of agreeing about abstract doctrines, as if mere agreement about what constitutes "the right ideas" is really something of a profound order. Rather, what is primary is that disciples cultivate together long-suffering humility and care. Doctrinal disagreements will, no doubt, crop up, but they are not a threat to the essence of faith if the communal priorities remain focused on obedience to Jesus' ethics of forgiveness and mutual servanthood. Differences within the community can only be resolved over time once its unity of purpose (to *be* the gospel for all to see) is insisted upon as the fundamental basis for it. Those who would make some version of abstract doctrinal "purity" the basis for unity between Christians will never achieve the latter—or the former, either. "Faith without works is dead."

4:11—5:6: Admonitions Against Judging Others, Boasting, and Avarice

James follows his call to humility and repentance with three admonitions. First, in 4:11–12, he returns to the issue of the tongue, especially as it is misused to pronounce judgment on others. Next, in verses 13–17, he turns his attention again to wealthy Christians whose business dealings cause them to become arrogant, while they neglect to "do good." He denounces their boastful arrogance regarding their grand mercantile plans (which he straightforwardly calls "wicked"), as meanwhile they fail to notice the needs of their brothers and sisters in the faith. And, lastly, before he makes a final appeal to his hearers to be long-suffering and to endure in their trials, he utters his harshest, most unsparing, reproach yet of the rich (5:1–6).

h. *Do Not Judge One Another (4:11–12)*

¹¹ Μὴ καταλαλεῖτε ἀλλήλων, ἀδελφοί· ὁ καταλαλῶν ἀδελφοῦ ἢ κρίνων τὸν ἀδελφὸν αὐτοῦ καταλαλεῖ νόμου καὶ κρίνει νόμον· εἰ δὲ νόμον κρίνεις, οὐκ εἶ ποιητὴς νόμου ἀλλὰ κριτής. ¹² εἷς ἐστιν νομοθέτης καὶ κριτής, ὁ δυνάμενος σῶσαι καὶ ἀπολέσαι· σὺ δὲ τίς εἶ, ὁ κρίνων τὸν πλησίον;

¹¹*Do not speak against one another, brothers. Whoever speaks against a brother or judges a brother speaks against Law and judges Law; if you judge Law, you are not a doer of Law, but a judge. ¹²There is one Lawgiver and judge, he who has power to save and destroy. But who are you who judge your neighbor?*

Echoing Jesus ("Judge not, that you may not be judged; for by whatever verdict you pass judgment you shall be judged, and in whatever measure you measure it shall be meted out to you"; Matt 7:1–2), James warns his hearers not to pronounce judgment on one another. In communities fraught with divisiveness and doctrinal wrangling, one can easily imagine the temptation to condemn and anathematize others (as we saw in our discussion of 3:1–12 above). But, as Jesus had taught and James reiterates, the *individual* disciple has no license or right to pronounce *any* verdict on another, and especially not on fellow members of the community of disciples. If there has to be correction within the community, Jesus provided a three-step method of settling all such matters, according to Matthew 18:15–20:

> [*First step*:] Now, if your brother sins, go and remonstrate with him, between you and him privately. If he listens to you, you gain your brother; if, though, he does not listen,

> [*Second step*:] take one or two others along with you, so that everything that is said may be confirmed by the mouths of two or three witnesses; if, though, he refuses to listen to them,

[*Third and final step*:] tell it to the assembly; and if he refuses to listen even to the assembly, let him be to you as the gentile or the tax-collector.

Amen, I tell you, whatever things you bind on the earth will have been bound in heaven, and whatever things you unbind on the earth will have been unbound in heaven. Again, [amen,] I tell you that if two among you agree on earth concerning everything they request, whatever it is, it shall come to pass for them, coming from my Father in the heavens. For where there are two or three who have gathered in my name, I am there in their midst.

Only after following the process through to the very end with no success, then and only then does the *gathered community together* ("two or three") make the decision to send an erring disciple away. In other words, *no single individual* has a right to judge, but the entire community, if a dire situation demands it, may exercise judgment *because*—says Christ in Matthew 18:20—*and only because he, Jesus, is there in their midst*. He is identified with the *community* itself. Which is to say, *he* is acknowledged to be the one true Judge. Even so, Matthew follows this pericope with the parable of the servant who refused to forgive his fellow servant (Matt 18:21–34), which begins with this very short introductory story:

Then Peter approached and said to [Jesus], "Lord, how many times will my brother sin against me and I shall forgive him? As many as seven times?" Jesus says to him, "I tell you, not as many as seven times, but as many as seventy times seven. (Matt 18:21–22)

The point of that brief introductory story and the parable that follows is that forgiveness is *always* possible, even after multiple failures.

The problem with an individual presuming to deliver a "verdict" about another is that, besides being intrinsically absurd, the potential for the forgiveness of sins is consequently reduced, usually through the self-righteousness of the one venturing to judge. In doctrinal disputes, such as the one occupying James's attention in chapter two, in which dialogue and mutual—perhaps lengthy—listening is needed, any temptation to judge, condemn, and anathematize ought to be restrained altogether. Judgment should have to do with actual sin only, not the policing of doctrinal disputes. The latter should be worked through with forbearance and charity. And judgment is never for individuals to exercise at all.

James strengthens the argument with reference to the Law. The one Lawgiver and Judge, he declares, is God or Christ. You who pretend to judge, he says, do not qualify. Do not presume, then, to seat yourself in God's throne—it's already occupied. If you presume to "judge" another, you are in effect judging the Law of the one Lawgiver—and that because it was precisely the one Lawgiver who told you that you are *not* to judge. Thus the awful words: "But who are you who judge your neighbor?" It's a convicting appeal that James makes to the believer, echoing a similar rebuke of presumptuousness in Psalm 50. In the latter, the psalmist describes a scene of judgment in which God addresses those who stand before him. Significantly, presaging James, what he reproaches in them is their abusive speech—evil words, deceit, and slander. And also, it seems, they indulge in an illusion that they speak on God's behalf—in "judgment," if you will—presuming that God is "like" them.

> "You give your mouth free rein for evil,
>   and your tongue frames deceit.
> You sit and speak against your brother;
>   you slander your own mother's son.
> These things you have done and I have been silent;
> *you thought that I was one like yourself.*
> But now I rebuke you, and lay the charge before you . . . ."
> (Ps 50:19–21; emphasis mine)

Again, given that such judgmental and condemning behavior erupts whenever divisions and factions come about, James's exhortation to warring "brothers" entirely fits within the larger frame of the epistle's concerns. He is continuing, without break, the interlinked chain of his criticism.

i. *Boasting of One's Plans While Neglecting to Do Good (4:13–17)*

[13] Ἄγε νῦν οἱ λέγοντες· Σήμερον ἢ αὔριον πορευσόμεθα εἰς τήνδε τὴν πόλιν καὶ ποιήσομεν ἐκεῖ ἐνιαυτὸν καὶ ἐμπορευσόμεθα καὶ κερδήσομεν· [14] οἵτινες οὐκ ἐπίστασθε τὸ τῆς αὔριον ποία ἡ ζωὴ ὑμῶν· ἀτμὶς γάρ ἐστε ἡ πρὸς ὀλίγον φαινομένη, ἔπειτα καὶ ἀφανιζομένη· [15] ἀντὶ τοῦ λέγειν ὑμᾶς· Ἐὰν ὁ κύριος θελήσῃ, καὶ ζήσομεν καὶ ποιήσομεν τοῦτο ἢ ἐκεῖνο. [16] νῦν δὲ καυχᾶσθε ἐν ταῖς ἀλαζονείαις ὑμῶν· πᾶσα καύχησις τοιαύτη πονηρά ἐστιν. [17] εἰδότι οὖν καλὸν ποιεῖν καὶ μὴ ποιοῦντι, ἁμαρτία αὐτῷ ἐστιν.

¹³Come now, you who say, "Today or tomorrow we shall journey into this city, and spend a year there, and engage in commerce, and make a profit": ¹⁴You who do not know what your life will be like on the morrow—for you are a vapor, appearing for a short while and then vanishing—¹⁵You should instead say, "If the Lord will it, we shall both live and also do this or that." ¹⁶But now, in your pretentiousness, you boast; all such boasting is wicked. ¹⁷Therefore, when someone knows to do the good and does not do it, it is sin for him.

James once again addresses those within the Christian communities who are wealthy—specifically, he addresses those "who engage in commerce" and harbor grand schemes to "make a profit."

I cited Martin Hengel's essay in the Introduction as one that has had some influence on my views. I will note here that he proposed an elaborate thesis concerning these very verses.[3] His opinion, which I find intriguing but not convincing enough for me to accept, is that James was again taking aim at Paul—in this case, Paul's missionary strategy, his tendency to "boast" of his plans, and his reliance on wealthy patrons to assist him in these endeavors. Hengel summarizes his hypothesis this way:

> The travel plans, encompassing great geographical and temporal space, which Paul himself outlines in his letters, not least in connection with his combined Jerusalem-Rome-Spain project (cf. Rom. 15:14ff.; 2 Cor. 10:13ff.), come suspiciously close to the intentions James imputes to his plan-forging "businessmen" traveling to (large) cities . . . Paul was dependent in his strategy upon the assistance of well-to-do friends, among other things perhaps in order to raise money for the relatively high rent of the "School of Tyrannus" in Ephesus (Acts 19:9), for passages by ship with several participants, or for lodging in Rome. (Acts 28:30)

Although I believe (as did Hengel) that James was addressing communities wrangling over a dubious interpretation of Paul's teaching, Hengel's hypothesis here strikes me as unnecessarily complicated. It is certainly worth weighing, but I opt for a simpler explanation of 4:13–17 below.

3. Hengel, "The Letter of James as Anti-Pauline Polemic," in *The Writings of St. Paul: A Norton Critical Edition* (2nd ed.), edited by Wayne A. Meeks and John T. Fitzgerald (New York: W. W. Norton, 2007), cf. 246–48.

Simply stated, early church communities appear to have reflected the same class differences one would have found in the general population surrounding them: slaves, the poor, tradespersons of all sorts, the upwardly mobile (in Corinth, for example), and the wealthy. Concerning the church at Corinth, Paul could write that "not many [of its members were] wise according to flesh, not many powerful, not many well-born" (1 Cor 1:26). And yet, ten chapters on, he is dealing with a serious problem that threatened to drive a wedge between groups in the church along class lines—and, most alarmingly for Paul, this rift had become especially problematic when the community gathered to share a feast (what was known as an *agape*— i.e., "love"—feast) and to celebrate the Lord's Supper (the sign of unity). Consequently, he treats their sacramental meal as a parody. Paul's rebuke is scathing:

> When you convene in the same place, therefore, it is not to eat the Lord's supper; for, in eating, each proceeds with his own supper, and one man goes hungry while another is besotted. For do you not, in fact, have households for eating and drinking in? Or do you despise God's assembly and humiliate those who have nothing? What should I tell you? Shall I praise you? In this matter, I offer no praise. (1 Cor 11:20–22)

What this passage seems to indicate is that Paul's communities were not as "communistic" in practice as were the original Jerusalem community— James's church and the mother church of all churches, in other words (Acts 2:44–45; 4:32–35).[4] The class divisions of the surrounding society appear to have been carried over wholesale into the Corinthian church's life, even if—as we can suppose—wealthier members might have also assisted those in need on occasion.

James has become aware that there are similar divisions along class lines within the communities he exhorts (which may perhaps have included that same church in Corinth), and that—as he sees it—the rich are to blame for it. If the "communistic" Jerusalem church was his model, it's quite possible that he would have viewed the wealthy as most at fault. In this, he follows closely in his brother's footsteps. As we will see in 5:1–6 below, he accuses the rich of directly practicing injustice. But, in this passage, he addresses two other related offenses of the rich: *arrogance* and *neglect*.

---

4. An excellent book on the early church's economic life, spanning the apostolic and early patristic periods, is Roman Montero, *All Things in Common: The Economic Practices of the Early Christians* (Eugene, OR: Resource, 2017).

They are *arrogant* and boastful about their commercial schemes, while *neglecting* to do good to those who are less fortunate than themselves: "Therefore, when someone knows to do the good and does not do it, it is sin for him" (4:17). In context, it seems that James may have been distressed to learn that certain rich merchants in the congregation not only were not "doing good" for the poorer members, but that they were even guilty of a practical callousness towards them. Lancelot Andrewes, the great Anglican divine and one of the translators of the King James Version of the Bible, made explicit James's point in a sermon he preached on 1 Timothy 6:17–19: "For having wealth and wherewithal to 'do good', if you do it not, talk not of faith, for you have no faith in you."[5] James, as we know already, would have seen in such neglect a "faith" belied by its lack of works, or—simply—a "dead" faith.

The passage is reminiscent somewhat of Jesus' parable about the rich man and the poor beggar, Lazarus (Luke 16:19–31). The rich man in the story eats daily his sumptuous meals and meanwhile neglects the beggar on his doorstep, while even knowing his name (as seems to be indicated by his calling out to Abraham from his torments to send Lazarus to him with a little water). The image in the parable is intentionally ludicrous; and yet James is indicating that something along similar lines is actually occurring right in the midst of ostensibly Christian communities. The rich are preoccupied with business and gain, and the needs of the poor are being neglected.

For James, then, the question must have been: Just what sort of "gospel" is it that these rich Christians actually think they believe in? The answer to that question, it seems, is already to be found back in the second chapter. The sort of "gospel" that could very well ease the consciences of the well-to-do, to the disregard of compassionate action, would be one which elevates a routine "faith" and downgrades proactive moral "works" as superfluous for salvation (in other words, a religion antithetical to what Jesus had taught in the parable of Matthew 25:31–46). Disparity between rich and poor has, of course, been a recurring problem throughout the church's history—despite the fact that equality between believers and churches was an apostolic ideal. Class divisions have been with us always, often to the

5. Online at: Project Canterbury, Library of Anglo-Catholic Theology: *Lancelot Andrewes, Works, Sermons, Volume Five*, 3–53, "Certain Sermons Preached at Sundry Times Upon Several Occasions, Sermon I (Preached at St. Mary's Hospital, on the Tenth of April, being Wednesday in Easter-week, A.D. MDLXXXVIII)"; Transcribed by Dr. Marianne Dorman, 2002 (http://anglicanhistory.org/lact/andrewes/v5/misc1.html).

shame of the church and despite the voices of her greatest saints and prophets. We can witness the unabashed justifying of wealth and privilege today among many American Christians—among those who mix Christianity with a zeal for laissez-faire capitalism, for instance, or who try to find some sort of impossible compatibility between Jesus and Ayn Rand. What James was protesting in his epistle two millennia ago should be instantly recognizable to us (if we have eyes to see it for what it is) because—in a different cultural guise, of course—the problem is still with us.

If then there is in the background, as Hengel suggested, any link to the sort of missionary activities Paul engaged in, it isn't directly obvious. What is evident is that there is arrogance and neglect on the part of the wealthy, and so James is once more bringing us back in this passage to the theme of what constitutes true religion: "Pure and undefiled religion before the God and Father is this: to watch over orphans and widows in their affliction, to keep oneself unstained by the cosmos" (1:27). The wealthy, he is saying, are stained by the cosmos (with their plans and their boasting), and the "orphans and widows" and others less fortunate are overlooked.

James also reminds the rich that they have a quite natural cause to be humble and to do right. Verses 14–16 remind them that they, like everyone else, will die: "You who do not know what your life will be like on the morrow—for you are a vapor, appearing for a short while and then vanishing—you should instead say, 'If the Lord will it, we shall both live and also do this or that.' But now, in your pretentiousness, you boast; all such boasting is wicked." That is to say, that *because* they "are a vapor" doomed to "vanish," hemmed in by mortality and whose very lives are the gift of God, they should wake up and realize that their great plans are not really in their own hands at all. Or, as the book of Proverbs has it, "A man's mind plans his way, but the LORD directs his steps." (Prov 16:9) Even more to the point, with the possibility of our death always nearer than we care to believe, all pretentious boasting is evil. It distracts us from reality. It is delusional. It is to be intentionally guarded against (and thereby we can keep ourselves "unstained by the cosmos").

And about this very tendency, Jesus warned us in a parable:

> And [Jesus] said to them, "Be wary and guard against all greed, because one's life does not consist in the abundance of his possessions." And he told them a parable saying, "The land of a certain rich man yielded well, and he reasoned with himself, 'What shall I do? For I have nowhere to gather in my fruits?' And he said, 'I shall

do this: I shall pull down my granaries and build larger ones and I shall gather there all my grain and goods, and I shall say to my soul, "Soul, you have many goods stored up for many years; take your ease, eat, drink, make merry." But God said to him, 'Fool, this night they demand your soul from you; the things you prepare, then, whose will they be?' Thus is the one storing up treasure for himself but not being rich toward God." (Luke 12:15–21)

It is verse 17—"Therefore, when someone knows to do the good and does not do it, it is sin for him"—that forms the "hinge" which opens immediately into the next passage:

j. Warnings to the Rich (5:1–6)

⁵·¹ Ἄγε νῦν οἱ πλούσιοι, κλαύσατε ὀλολύζοντες ἐπὶ ταῖς ταλαιπωρίαις ὑμῶν ταῖς ἐπερχομέναις. ² ὁ πλοῦτος ὑμῶν σέσηπεν, καὶ τὰ ἱμάτια ὑμῶν σητόβρωτα γέγονεν, ³ ὁ χρυσὸς ὑμῶν καὶ ὁ ἄργυρος κατίωται, καὶ ὁ ἰὸς αὐτῶν εἰς μαρτύριον ὑμῖν ἔσται καὶ φάγεται τὰς σάρκας ὑμῶν· ὡς πῦρ ἐθησαυρίσατε ἐν ἐσχάταις ἡμέραις. ⁴ ἰδοὺ ὁ μισθὸς τῶν ἐργατῶν τῶν ἀμησάντων τὰς χώρας ὑμῶν ὁ ἀφυστερημένος ἀφ᾽ ὑμῶν κράζει, καὶ αἱ βοαὶ τῶν θερισάντων εἰς τὰ ὦτα Κυρίου Σαβαὼθ εἰσεληλύθασιν· ⁵ ἐτρυφήσατε ἐπὶ τῆς γῆς καὶ ἐσπαταλήσατε, ἐθρέψατε τὰς καρδίας ὑμῶν ἐν ἡμέρᾳ σφαγῆς. ⁶ κατεδικάσατε, ἐφονεύσατε τὸν δίκαιον. οὐκ ἀντιτάσσεται ὑμῖν;

⁵·¹*Come now, you who are rich, weep, howling out at the miseries that are coming for you:* ²*Your riches have spoiled and your garments have become moth-eaten;* ³*Your gold and silver have corroded, and their corrosion will serve as testimony against you and will eat your flesh like fire. You have kept treasure in the last days.* ⁴*Look: The wages of the workers who have reaped your lands, which have been unfairly held back by you, clamor aloud, and the outcries of those who have reaped have entered the ears of the Lord Sabaoth.* ⁵*You lived on the earth in dainty luxury and self-indulgence. You have gorged your hearts on a day of slaughter.* ⁶*You have condemned—have murdered—the upright man; he does not oppose you.*

Although it is often assumed that these harsh verses (and also the passage immediately preceding this one) are directed at "worldly" rich men whose depredations have victimized followers of Jesus, it seems more likely that James's prophetic denunciation is leveled at those who are wealthy and who profess faith in Christ. It is sometimes pointed out that 5:1–6 is not an explicit call to repentance, but a straightforward condemnation of the rich, in effect sealing their doom with a fierce malediction. No repentance seems possible, it is contended, for those whom James denounces; the admonition is not urging repentance, it is argued, but only pronouncing an indictment. I disagree with this argument. My own opinion is that James, in fact, is so inflexible in his severity *precisely because he intends to mortify his hearers and thereby bring them to their senses.* It is an appeal camouflaged as condemnation.

James's epistle was not written to be read outside the community of disciples, so it would seem likely that the *"you* who are rich" whom he addresses are persons who would, in fact, actually hear these words read out loud in the assembly. The assumption that this is a general reproof, composed for the edification of the persecuted but having no effect on those persons being reproved (the latter not even being present to hear it), seems improbable to me, not to mention pointless. Rather, James means to hit hard the consciences of those who most need to hear it and to change their behavior drastically. He wounds them in order to heal. He is, first and foremost, a pastor—not a critic of society at large. The call to repentance has already been issued in 4:1–10 and, in less direct terms, again in 4:17 immediately before the present passage—that "hinge" verse, as I referred to it above. We should also continue to bear in mind that James's view of the character of God, as we have seen from the very first chapter of his letter, is that his is one of perfect goodness, long-suffering, and willingness to forgive. If James now uses unyieldingly blunt and tough language, it is not meant merely to condemn, but to bring about a change of heart (cf. 5:19–20).

It is worth recalling, should we regard James's words as too severe and unrelenting, the story of Jesus' encounter with the rich young man in Matthew 19:16–22:

> And look: Someone approaching him said, "Teacher, what good thing may I do in order that I may have the life of the Age?" And he said to him, "Why do you question me concerning the good? One there is who is good. But if you wish to enter into life keep

the commandments." He says to him, "Which ones?" And Jesus said, "You shall not murder, you shall not commit adultery, you shall not steal, you shall not bear false witness, honor father and mother, and love your neighbor as yourself." The young man says to him, "All of these I have kept; what am I still lacking?" Jesus said to him, "If you wish to be perfect, go sell your possessions and give to the poor, and you shall have a treasury in the heavens, and come follow me." But the young man, hearing the counsel, went away in sorrow, for he was one who had many possessions.

What we should note is that Jesus does not chase after the young man. He merely states his demanding expectations if the man truly wishes to become Jesus' follower—which, in effect, means to become "perfect." To "be perfect" is, in fact, the very definition of what it is the disciple should seek to become, as Jesus had taught earlier in the same Gospel: "So be perfect, as your Heavenly Father is perfect" (Matt 5:48). This is not depicted as an impossible demand, even if it is a hard one. Within the overall context of Matthew 5:43–48, as we may recall, "perfection" or "completion" or "maturity" (τέλειος) means to be "perfect in love" or "perfect in showing care" or "perfect in doing good to others." And it means precisely the same thing, we can presume, in Matthew 19 with Jesus' words to the young rich man. In other words, Jesus was telling the rich man that his riches were keeping him from loving his neighbor, and thus from emulating the Father's perfect love for all, and that the road to such perfection (which is the road a follower of Jesus is meant to walk) required him to give freely to those in need.

But, although Jesus didn't pursue the rich man, he nonetheless offered a reason to have hope even for the rich to his disciples. Right after the young man's sorrowful departure, we read:

And Jesus said to his disciples, "Amen, I tell you that it will be hard for a rich man to enter into the Kingdom of the heavens. And again I tell you, it is easier for a camel to enter in through the eye of a needle than for a rich man to enter into the Kingdom of God." But on hearing this the disciples were greatly astonished, saying, "Can any of them then be saved?" And, looking directly at them, Jesus said to them, "For men this is impossible, but for God all things are possible." (Matt 19:23–26)

In summary, Jesus does not take back his demands. They remain firm and unyielding. If one wants in all seriousness to follow him, then one must know the radical nature of his calling—that it will entail an earnest pursuit of "perfection" in love. And that, in turn, will mean not hoarding the goods one has within his or her power to share with those in need. That was a standard Jesus put before his earliest followers, it was the standard for James's community in Jerusalem, and it is the standard James sets before his hearers in his epistle.

James's threat of impending judgment in verses 1–3, then, is thus a wake-up call to his hearers. He will not chase after them with a compromised call, but he is willing to speak roughly to them—as Jesus would have done—if it will jolt some of them to change their behavior. Some who are rich are in peril, he is warning them, lulled into a state of spiritual lassitude by a "gospel" of "faith without [the necessity of] works." He means to shake them up, using language reminiscent of his brother's warnings:

> Do not store up treasures for yourself on the earth, where moth and rust destroy, and where thieves penetrate by digging and steal; rather, store up for yourself treasure in Heaven, where neither moth nor rust destroys, and where thieves neither penetrate by digging nor steal; for where your treasure is, there your heart will also be. The lamp of the body is the eye. Thus if your eye be pure your entire body will be radiant; but if your eye be baleful your entire body will be dark. So if the light within you is darkness, how very great the darkness. No one can be a slave to two lords; for either he will hate the one and love the other, or he will stand fast by the one and disdain the other. You cannot be a slave both to God and to Mammon. (Matt 6:19–24)

James 5:2, in particular, echoes Jesus' exhortation to store up treasure "where neither moth nor rust destroys": "Your riches have spoiled and your garments have become moth-eaten." There could not be a sharper rebuke for those who would, one assumes, know these sayings of the Lord. It is a warning that their treasure is *not* "in heaven," and that they have *not* heeded Christ in the most basic matters. They are "slaves" of "Mammon" rather than of God, and they have failed even to recognize their dangerous condition.

Verses 4–6 are redolent with biblical passages that warn the rich and threaten them with judgment. Verse 4 ("The wages of the workers who have reaped your lands, which have been unfairly held back by you . . .") has for its foundation such texts as Leviticus 19:13: "You shall not oppress your neighbor or rob him. The wages of a hired servant shall not remain with you all night until the morning" (cf. Deut 24:14–15). In other words, wages are to be paid promptly and fully, and never "held back." When James says that these same held-back wages "clamor aloud, and the outcries of those who have reaped have entered the ears of the Lord Sabaoth" (or "Lord of (the heavenly) armies" (an image of approaching judgment) he echoes at once both Deuteronomy 24:15—". . . lest [the poor man] cry against you to the LORD, and it be sin to you"— and, even more terribly, the words of God to murderous Cain: "The voice of your brother's blood is crying to me from the ground" (Gen 4:10). The theme of impending judgment is underscored in verse 5, with its reference to "a day of slaughter" (cf. Jer 12:3). And verse 6 ("You have condemned—have murdered—the upright man; he does not oppose you") again moves us to think of Cain and also of the oppression and murder of "the righteous poor man" of Wisdom 2:10–20 (a text also associated in Christian tradition with the death of Christ).

Again, it should go without saying that such threats of God's judgment have only one purpose, and that is to *warn* those to whom they are pronounced. James is not indulging in the kind of condemnation he has himself denounced in his letter. He is employing in prophetic style, as his last recourse, a sort of shock therapy. He wants his wealthy Christian hearers to wake up and see the truth of their precarious situation before God, to notice the neglected poor in their midst, to alter course, to shoulder their responsibilities, to regard their goods as gifts to be distributed and not hoarded, and to become disciples who actually and earnestly *follow* Jesus' teachings—and not just pay him or rote doctrines about him lip service. In short, James's exhortations constitute an extended denunciation of glaring hypocrisy. And in this, as in all things, his exemplar was his brother and Lord.

5:7–12: An Appeal for Long-suffering and Restraint in Speech

⁷ Μακροθυμήσατε οὖν, ἀδελφοί, ἕως τῆς παρουσίας τοῦ κυρίου. ἰδοὺ ὁ γεωργὸς ἐκδέχεται τὸν τίμιον καρπὸν τῆς γῆς, μακροθυμῶν ἐπ' αὐτῷ ἕως λάβῃ πρόϊμον καὶ ὄψιμον. ⁸ μακροθυμήσατε καὶ ὑμεῖς, στηρίξατε τὰς καρδίας ὑμῶν, ὅτι ἡ παρουσία τοῦ κυρίου ἤγγικεν. ⁹ μὴ στενάζετε, ἀδελφοί, κατ' ἀλλήλων, ἵνα μὴ κριθῆτε· ἰδοὺ ὁ κριτὴς πρὸ τῶν θυρῶν ἔστηκεν. ¹⁰ ὑπόδειγμα λάβετε, ἀδελφοί, τῆς κακοπαθίας καὶ τῆς μακροθυμίας τοὺς προφήτας, οἳ ἐλάλησαν ἐν τῷ ὀνόματι κυρίου. ¹¹ ἰδοὺ μακαρίζομεν τοὺς ὑπομείναντας· τὴν ὑπομονὴν Ἰὼβ ἠκούσατε, καὶ τὸ τέλος κυρίου εἴδετε, ὅτι

πολύσπλαγχνός ἐστιν ὁ κύριος καὶ οἰκτίρμων. ¹²Πρὸ πάντων δέ, ἀδελφοί μου, μὴ ὀμνύετε, μήτε τὸν οὐρανὸν μήτε τὴν γῆν μήτε ἄλλον τινὰ ὅρκον· ἤτω δὲ ὑμῶν τὸ Ναὶ ναὶ καὶ τὸ Οὒ οὔ, ἵνα μὴ ὑπὸ κρίσιν πέσητε.

⁷*So, brothers, be long-suffering until the arrival of the Lord. Look: The farmer awaits the precious fruit of the earth, remaining patient over it until it receives the early and the late rains. ⁸You be patient too, strengthen your hearts, for the Lord's arrival has drawn near. ⁹Do not murmur against one another, brothers, so that you might not be judged—look: The judge is standing before the doors! ¹⁰Brothers, take the prophets who spoke in the name of the Lord for an example of suffering evil and of patience. ¹¹Look: We consider those who persevere blissful. You have heard of Job's endurance and you have seen the ending that came from the Lord—that the Lord is lavishly compassionate and merciful. ¹²But before all else, my brothers, do not swear—neither by the heaven nor by the earth nor by any other object of oaths; rather let your "Yes" be "Yes" and your "No" be "No," so that you may not fall under judgment.*

The Greek word μακροθυμία (*makrothumia*) means "long passion" and suggests the restraining of one's impatient "passions"—anger, frustration, despondency, and so on—until something which is anticipated, which requires forbearance as one waits, finally materializes. The word appears three times in verses 7 and 8 above (and will show up a fourth time in verse 10): "So, brothers, be long-suffering (Μακροθυμήσατε) until the arrival of the Lord. Look: The farmer awaits the precious fruit of the earth, remaining patient (μακροθυμῶν) over it until it receives the early and the late rains. You be patient (μακροθυμήσατε) too, strengthen your hearts, for the Lord's arrival has drawn near." In our translation of the text, the same word is rendered once as "long-suffering" and twice as "patient," but what we have here is an emphatic encouragement to "suffer long" with some burdensome or toilsome situation until one has completed a necessary task.

James has just uttered his harshest words in the entire epistle, directed at the rich in their midst, but now he addresses the entire community of believers, exhorting them not to indulge in "murmuring" against one another or "swearing," but to carry on their efforts in the proper frame of mind. The present passage should be read as picking up directly from what has preceded it, which is indicated by the word "so" in verse 7 (οὖν—a word which can also be translated as "therefore" or "then"). In other words, James has strongly assured his hearers that he is well aware that there are inequities among them and that a number of the poorer members endure injustices from wealthier members in their communities. He has made it publicly clear before the gathered assemblies that these injustices must cease, that the wealthier members must repent of their arrogant boastfulness and neglect of the poor, and that otherwise they can expect a harsh judgment (thus the preceding passage). But now, assuming that his words have struck a chord, he appeals to all the members that there should be no bitter talk and damning recriminations. *So, therefore*—he writes—there should be the exercising of long-suffering towards one another and constant mindfulness that the Lord's "arrival" is at hand. James, like all early Christians, expected the return of Christ to occur during his own time ("the Lord's arrival has *drawn near* . . . . The Judge *is standing* before the doors!"; vss. 8 and 9). James's basic point is straightforward: all must stand before the Judge (by which is probably meant Christ), who already has been described by James as the *one* Lawgiver and Judge in 4:12, and therefore all believers should be willing to exercise charity towards one another for the duration and perform the good works to which they are called, without "murmuring" against one another or grandly "swearing."

The image of the *working* farmer, bearing up under his labors, is a reminder of James's stress on works. The agricultural image of "the early and late rains," which refer respectively to the rainy seasons in October and April, suggests that the believers' patience may, in fact, need to last for as long as it takes for "precious fruit" to appear (cf. Deut 11:14; Jer 5:24; Joel 2:23). The agricultural metaphor, in fact, reminds us of Jesus' frequent use of the same sort of farming analogies in his parables.

As suggested, it would seem that the key verses in this passage, given James's exhortations in past chapters regarding the tongue and the contentions in these communities, are verses 9 and 12: "Do not murmur against one another [i.e., blame one another], brothers, so that you might not be judged . . . . But before all else, my brothers, do not swear: neither by the heaven nor by the earth nor by any other object of oaths; rather let your 'Yes' be 'Yes' and your 'No' be 'No,' so that you may not fall under judgment." These appeals continue the theme of approaching judgment, and both verses draw from Jesus' teachings—verse 9 from such sayings as Matthew 7:1–5, and verse 12 is almost a direct quote from Matthew 5:34–37:

> Whereas I tell you not to swear at all: neither by heaven, inasmuch as it is God's throne; nor by the earth, inasmuch as it is the footstool of his feet; nor by Jerusalem, inasmuch as it is the Great King's city;—neither swear by your own head, inasmuch as you cannot make a single hair white or black. Rather, let your utterance be "Yes, yes," "No, no"; because it is from the roguish man that anything more extravagant than this comes.

Since this exhortation might possibly refer back to matters related to our discussion of 3:1–12 above (see the comments there regarding Paul's anathemas of Galatians 1:8–9), it is worth mentioning that a person pronouncing an anathema against others could be considered as "swearing" in the sense that James, following Jesus, here censures. What Jesus and James condemn is the pronunciation of a (pseudo) verdict, uttered perhaps with impatience and excessiveness. It is not implausible that some who saw themselves as faithfully emulating Paul's style might have adopted a propensity for denouncing with the force of an oath those with whom they disagreed doctrinally. If so, James's warning may be intentionally pointed here.

Verses 10–11 hold before the eyes of James's audience the examples of the prophets and of Job in particular. The prophets are models "of suffering evil" (κακοπαθίας; bearing up under hardship) and—once again—"of patience" (μακροθυμίας; long-suffering). This mention of suffering might refer to the persecution of Christian communities. Paul, after all, was in prison (if the proposed dating we have assumed is correct), and so we can imagine that there were other related hardships imposed on Christians by Roman authorities or those in the general population who despised them. But that need not explain, or at least exhaust, James's meaning here. Any reference to active or violent persecution in the letter is subdued at best, and the few instances where it might be pertinent can be explained by something less distressing in nature. James may, in fact, still be reflecting on the hardships poorer members in the communities undergo through neglect—a theme that has energized him more than once already (2:5–7; 4:13–17; 5:1–6). Still, bringing up the prophets as exemplars of endurance echoes Jesus in Matthew 5:11–12, which refers specifically to persecution: "How blissful you when they reproach you, and persecute you and falsely accuse you of every evil for my sake: rejoice and be glad, for your reward in the heavens is great; for thus they persecuted the prophets before you" (cf. Acts 7:52). Even so, James may have lesser hardships in mind than the traumas of violent persecution.

Nor was Job a victim of violent persecution, but of suffering both inner and outer trials. Verse 11, which brings up Job, mirrors some of the earliest verses of the letter. Compare 1:12 ("How blissful the man who endures trial, because—having become proven—he will receive the crown of the life that [God] has promised to those who love him") with verse 11 ("We consider those who persevere blissful. You have heard of Job's endurance and you have seen the ending that came from the Lord: that the Lord is lavishly compassionate and merciful"). Recalling that Job's trials were not only the loss of his health, family, and property, but also the wrestling of his inner man with incomprehension, the increasingly hostile arguments posed by false friends, and his crumbling sense of personal righteousness, we can suppose that James's praise of Job for his perseverance is relevant on more than one level. And, yet again, James stresses that God is absolutely good in his nature—he is "lavishly compassionate and merciful"—which Job experienced in the restoration of his material goods at the conclusion of his story. We can be certain, however, that James does not mean to suggest that his readers will receive any such material gains for their perseverance— nothing of the kind was ever promised by Jesus to his followers. But, as verse 11 puts it, through perseverance they *can* hope to receive "the crown of the *life* that he has promised to those who love him"—which is one of the many metaphors in the New Testament for becoming "communicants in the divine nature" (2 Pet 1:4), the promise that "when he appears we shall be like him, because we shall see him as he is." (1 John 3:2)

5:13–20: *The Communal Life*

¹³ Κακοπαθεῖ τις ἐν ὑμῖν; προσευχέσθω· εὐθυμεῖ τις; ψαλλέτω. ¹⁴ ἀσθενεῖ τις ἐν ὑμῖν; προσκαλεσάσθω τοὺς πρεσβυτέρους τῆς ἐκκλησίας, καὶ προσευξάσθωσαν ἐπ' αὐτὸν ἀλείψαντες αὐτὸν ἐλαίῳ ἐν τῷ ὀνόματι τοῦ κυρίου· ¹⁵ καὶ ἡ εὐχὴ τῆς πίστεως σώσει τὸν κάμνοντα, καὶ ἐγερεῖ αὐτὸν ὁ κύριος· κἂν ἁμαρτίας ᾖ πεποιηκώς, ἀφεθήσεται αὐτῷ. ¹⁶ ἐξομολογεῖσθε οὖν ἀλλήλοις τὰς ἁμαρτίας καὶ εὔχεσθε ὑπὲρ ἀλλήλων, ὅπως ἰαθῆτε. πολὺ ἰσχύει δέησις δικαίου ἐνεργουμένη. ¹⁷ Ἠλίας ἄνθρωπος ἦν ὁμοιοπαθὴς

ἡμῖν, καὶ προσευχῇ προσηύξατο τοῦ μὴ βρέξαι, καὶ οὐκ ἔβρεξεν ἐπὶ τῆς γῆς ἐνιαυτοὺς τρεῖς καὶ μῆνας ἕξ· ¹⁸ καὶ πάλιν προσηύξατο, καὶ ὁ οὐρανὸς ὑετὸν ἔδωκεν καὶ ἡ γῆ ἐβλάστησεν τὸν καρπὸν αὐτῆς.
¹⁹ Ἀδελφοί μου, ἐάν τις ἐν ὑμῖν πλανηθῇ ἀπὸ τῆς ἀληθείας καὶ ἐπιστρέψῃ τις αὐτόν, ²⁰ γινωσκέτω ὅτι ὁ ἐπιστρέψας ἁμαρτωλὸν ἐκ πλάνης ὁδοῦ αὐτοῦ σώσει ψυχὴν αὐτοῦ ἐκ θανάτου καὶ καλύψει πλῆθος ἁμαρτιῶν.

¹³*Is anyone among you suffering evil? Let him pray. Is anyone of good cheer? Let him sing psalms. ¹⁴Is anyone among you ill? Let him summon the elders of the assembly, and let them pray over him, having anointed him with oil in the name of the Lord. ¹⁵And the prayer of faith will save the one who is ailing, and the Lord will raise him up, and if he should be someone who has committed sins it will be forgiven him. ¹⁶Therefore fully acknowledge your sins to one another, and pray on one another's behalf, so that you might be healed. An upright man's petition, when it is put into effect, is very powerful. ¹⁷Elijah was a man, with feelings like ours, and he prayed a prayer that it might not rain, and no rain fell upon the earth for three years and six months; ¹⁸And again he prayed, and the sky gave rain, and the earth brought forth her fruit.*

¹⁹*My brothers, if anyone among you should stray from the truth, and some-one should turn him back, ²⁰Be aware that the one who turns a sinner back from the error of his way will save his soul from death and will cover over a multitude of sins.*

The concluding verses of James's letter lay emphasis on the sort of communal life that his readers should be cultivating among themselves. There is a notable stress on three features in particular: *mutual healing, mutual confession of sins,* and *mutual prayer.* The three are intertwined. When one seeks the prayer of healing, he or she should confess their sins; when the community confesses its sins, it is so the members can be healed through the prayers of one another. In short, James's idea of community is, to a great extent, *mutually therapeutic.* The Christian community exists, among other reasons, for the healing and integration of its members' spirits and bodies through their prayerful and supportive interaction. The gravest "sickness" James has confronted throughout his epistle has been that of being "two-souled"—that is to say, of not being inwardly united (1:8;

4:8). Or, as Augustine was to express it, "Our whole business in this life is to restore to health the eye of the heart whereby God may be seen" (*Sermo* 88.5.5). James is saying that each Christian's inner reintegration and health is empowered through the loving cooperation and relational bond of the church's members.

But first, in verse 13, James continues with the theme of speech from verse 12. Those who are "suffering evil" (Κακοπαθεῖ; cf. vs. 10) should pray— rather than, one supposes, "murmuring against one other" (vs. 9). Those who are cheerful (εὐθυμεῖ—"well-impassioned") should "sing psalms" (a word that can refer both to the canonical psalter and to early Christian hymnody)—possibly meaning they should do so rather than become diverted into "worldly" boasting (cf. 4:13–17). In both instances, one's tongue is redirected from the various forms of speech that self-centeredness fosters towards communion with God.

Verses 14–16 speak of communal support and mutual love. They and the other concluding verses are not merely tacked on at the letter's end as an afterthought, but *constitute a succinct expression of what James hopes to see in the churches to which he writes*. As mentioned above, he is concerned to encourage mutual healing, mutual confession of sins, and mutual prayer. And these are not easily teased apart in this passage.

Verses 14 and 15 emphasize healing. It is the responsibility of "the elders of the assembly" (τοὺς πρεσβυτέρους τῆς ἐκκλησίας), by which is meant the designated pastoral officers who were, in time, to become the "clerical orders" of the church (cf., for example, Acts 15:1), to exercise the ministry of anointing the sick with olive oil. During his own ministry, Jesus had sent out his apostles with oil for the sake of healing those to whom they proclaimed repentance (Mark 6:13). Olive oil was used for many purposes in the culture of that time—among other things, as food, as fuel for the lighting of lamps, as ointment for the skin, and as a medicament both internally and externally. The elders of each Christian assembly are meant to carry on the apostolic practice of anointing the sick and praying over them in the Lord's (Jesus') name.

Verse 15—"And the prayer of faith will save the one who is ailing, and the Lord will raise him up, and if he should be someone who has committed sins it will be forgiven him"—is meant to put us in mind of two levels of meaning at the same time (and here we can see James at his most nuanced). On one level, we have in mind the healings Christ performed during his ministry, which involved the raising up of the sick and even the dead to restored health and life (cf. Mk. 2:9; 5:41). But, on another level, James may very well intend by his use of the terms "save" (σώσει) and "raise . . . up" (ἐγερεῖ), both words in the future tense, a meaning more anagogical in nature as well. In other words, whether the sick person lives or dies in the present, his "salvation" (the perfect "cure") and "resurrection" are ultimately assured.

In those churches that have maintained the oldest traditions, the sacrament of anointing for healing has been restricted to those whose illnesses are considered to be life-threatening in nature. The rite usually involves confession and absolution, and it is considered a preparation for death as much as it is an intervention for possible physical and spiritual healing. One of the fundamental scriptural texts cited for this practice has been this verse from James. As such, it is a perfectly valid citation since it appears to be James's intention that the act of anointing the sick should be preparation for the real possibility of impending death. The sick man is anointed along with "the prayer of faith" and, confessing his sins, he can now die—if it is the Lord's will—in the certain hope of being "saved" from death and "raised up" to life in the Age to come. The profoundest "healing" is, in fact, the assurance that his sins "will be forgiven him."

James, along with early Christianity in general, recognized that there is an "infirmity" within each person that needs healing—one that lies deeper than the person's outward form. We can with justification assume that James understood Christ's works of healing as the early Fathers also did, literally as miraculous events and, figuratively, as much more than miraculous events. As the Gospel of John straightforwardly refers to them, they are *signs* of the fuller work Christ performs in those who come to him for "healing." This point cannot be stressed too strongly. When we read the accounts of Jesus healing the blind, deaf, dumb, lame, etc., casting out demons, and even defeating death, these healings represent the redemptive work of Christ—the ultimate "salvation" and "raising up" of his people.

One can see such an interpretation, for example, in homilies of the Fathers. They frequently apply the healing accounts to the lives of their hearers. Not only did Jesus heal the physically blind, for instance, but we ourselves are also inwardly "blind" until our "sight" is "restored" and we can "see" the light of Christ; we are the "deaf" who are healed so that we can "hear" the saving word; we are the "lepers" who are "cleansed" from the disease of ungoverned passions; we are the "lame" and "paralyzed" who are freed to "rise and follow" Christ in "the way," and so on. In other words, what Jesus did outwardly in his ministry, he continues to do inwardly in the depths of human hearts and minds.

I will cite a single example. If we look into early Christian homilies on Jesus' healing of the leper in Matthew 8:1–4, we frequently find spiritual applications of the story for the hearers. Origen, for instance, stresses that the leper's prayer ("Lord, if you wish, you are able to cleanse me") can beneficially be made our prayer as well: "Let us consider here, beloved brothers, if there be anyone that has the taint of leprosy in his soul, or the contamination of guilt in his heart? If he has, instantly adoring God, let him say to him: '*Lord, if you wish, you are able to cleanse me.*'" [6] With such interpretations as this one, the Fathers emphasized the deeper nature of Jesus' works as *signs* of the healing of the "inner man." James's statement that a sick person who receives the ministry of prayer and anointing will also have his or her sins forgiven is not far removed from this outlook at all. In both, the ministry of healing is interwoven with absolution and prayer.

After so much in this epistle that addresses the abuse of the tongue and the "wars" and divisions between Christians, James's emphasis now on mutual prayer and confession should be regarded as his proposed remedy. Verse 16 can be seen here as the pivotal one for the entire passage: "Therefore fully acknowledge your sins to one another, and pray on one another's behalf, so that you might be healed. An upright man's petition, when it is put into effect, is very powerful." Not only should confession of sins be a part of the prayer and anointing for the healing of the sick, but confession itself is to be practiced for the sake of the members' healing.

Again, healing is more than physical; it is spiritual restoration (cf. Heb 12:12–13). In the early church, such confession was a communal practice. This custom lies behind the exhortation of 1 John 1:9: "If we confess our sins, he is faithful and just, so that he may forgive us our sins and purge us of all iniquity" (and to be "purged of all iniquity" is, in fact, "salvation"). The *Didache* (which may have been written virtually any time between c. 50 and 150) is as explicit as James in its appeal: "In the congregation [ἐκκλησία] you shall confess your transgressions, and you shall not betake yourself to prayer with an evil conscience. This is the way of life" (*Did.* IV, 14)[7]. In James's letter, this practice has for its immediate backdrop the wrangling

6. The homily is included in M. F. Toal, trans. and ed., *The Sunday Sermons of the Great Fathers: Volume One: From the First Sunday of Advent to Quinquagesima* (London: Longmans, Green and Co., 1957), 301–2. Language updated.

7. *The Apostolic Fathers*, Vol. I, with an English translation by Kirsopp Lake (Cambridge, MA: Loeb Classical Library, 1912), 317. Language updated.

and mutual bitterness that he has censured so forcefully earlier. What can heal their wounds now, he is saying, is coming together to humble themselves, confess their wrongs, and pray as a united, reintegrated body.

James chooses the prophet Elijah as an example of prayerfulness. In verses 17–18, he describes the latter as praying for a drought (which was to last three and a half years), and then afterwards as praying for rain to heal the parched land. In actuality, 1 Kings 17:1–7 do not present Elijah as praying for the drought, although he does prophesy to the apostate King Ahab that there would be one. He is, however, described as instrumental through his prayers for the rain's return in 1 Kings 18:41–46. One can only conjecture why James chose Elijah to illustrate his point—the choice might have been customary, for instance, since Elijah's prayerfulness was no doubt considered paradigmatic. But, could it also possibly have been because Elijah's ministry had notably been exercised in a time of apostasy and impure religion? James's warnings throughout the epistle, after all, had been to counter infidelity in the congregations he addresses. It may be a stretch, but perhaps Elijah came readily to his mind when tackling the debasement of religion he saw there.

We come, then, to the final verses of the letter, and they may even be regarded as his rationale for having written it: "My brothers, if anyone among you should stray [πλανηθῇ = 'wander'] from the truth, and someone should turn him back [in the right direction], be aware that the one who turns a sinner back from the error [πλάνης = 'wandering'] of his way will save his soul from death and will cover over a multitude of sins [ἁμαρτιῶν = 'goings astray']." Since he has spent the entire epistle warning his readers that they have either strayed, or were on the point of straying, from the truth, he is now exhorting them to help keep one another on the right path. This should be the outcome of their mutual confession and prayer: to save one another from *wandering off* into error and sin. Such mutual effort is meritorious. We see similar such appeals in other early Christian texts: "Above all, have fervent love for one another, for love covers over a multitude of sins" (1 Pet 4:8); "Persevere in these things; for, in so doing, you will save both yourself and those listening to you" (1 Tim 4:16b–c); "Love unites us to God. Love covers a multitude of sins . . ." (1 *Clement* 49:5).[8] And, although James does not use the word "love" above (but see 2:8), it is the unsaid foundation for both these verses and of his entire epistle.

8. Ibid., 93.

It is not entirely clear in the Greek text just whose soul it is—that of the sinner or of the one turning the sinner back from wandering into error—that will thereby have his or her "multitude of sins" covered. I tend to think he means the sinner's. But, either way, "*love* covers a multitude of sins." James would not disagree with that summation. It is, after all, the sole purpose of his encyclical: to turn back those wandering into wrong paths and to save souls from the ways of death. That is the ultimate task of love and indeed of a loving pastor of souls.

Concluding Comments

By way of conclusion, and at the risk of being redundant, I would like to list a few salient points that have struck me in the course of writing this commentary. I could have listed more but, for the sake of simplicity, I think these few are sufficient.

1. **The Letter of James is far more cohesive as an epistle than is sometimes acknowledged.**

   The themes are closely interrelated. The issues of wealthy Christians and their treatment of poorer ones, sins of the tongue (especially among those assuming the role of "teachers"), and internal strife within the various communities that James addresses, hang together with his denunciation of a misunderstanding of Pauline doctrine.

   These various features of the letter fall into place as aspects of a single overriding concern when one assumes that the doctrine James condemns is one that, in its effects, undermines the "royal law—'You shall love your neighbor as yourself'" (2:8). A corrupted "gospel," one that guts the moral dimension of Christian life by stressing what Dietrich Bonhoeffer famously referred to as "cheap grace," could easily have led to the very abuses that James reprimands.

2. **We should not be troubled by the fact that the early leaders of the church didn't always see eye to eye.**

   As we have had occasion to note, it isn't clear how much James may have blamed Paul—whom he never mentions by name in the letter—for the faults of his followers. If we assume, as I do, that James is addressing communities either founded or impacted by Paul's teachings, we can suppose that he may have regarded Paul as a mixed blessing. He may have been quite aware of Paul's occasional lapses into intemperate speech, for example.

That Paul and James could have agreed on most essential points seems obvious when once we note (as I have in our discussion of the second chapter) that each of them uses the word "works" in a different way. Whereas Paul uses the word to speak of legalistic demands pertaining to outward ceremonial observances, James means—again—the "royal law" of practicing loving works towards one's neighbors. The blame for misconstruing Paul, I believe, did not lie with James, but with followers of Paul who had propagated an aberrant version of his teachings.

Be that as it may, James's criticisms of misconstrued Pauline doctrine should not vex us too much. Paul, after all, was even rougher on Peter in his Letter to the Galatians (and, by extension and rather more carefully, on James). What we should be able to accept is that differences between even the greatest apostolic figures are reflected in the New Testament, if we read the canon with care. What is praiseworthy about the canon is its capacity to hold these differences in tension. We might perhaps see, as a healthy consequence of appreciating these tensions, how it is possible that one New Testament author's perspective, taken out of its canonical context, can be exaggerated or abused without counterbalance or complement from other New Testament voices. We can be thankful, then, that James cautions us not to see Jesus' gospel as in any way opposed to the performance of good works, but that, in fact, it demands them.

3. **Faith without active love is dead.**

As noted in the commentary, James's argument in 2:26 is that "faith"—understood as "what one believes" or gives "creedal" assent to—is dead without the works or actions that confirm it as a deeper reality. And by "works," as we have said, James means the active love we demonstrate towards our neighbor.

His repeated criticisms regarding the rich and their neglect and mistreatment of the poor, the abusive use of the tongue, and the conflicts ripping apart the churches, are rooted in his conviction that the "gospel" they are affirming is one that has been perverted into a lifeless fideism, thereby undermining the foundational teachings of Jesus himself regarding the way of life his disciples should follow. Without active love and care for others, all their doctrinal wrangling is about as meaningful as Lilliput and Blefuscu arguing over which end of the egg to crack. Orthopraxy is the most basic level of orthodoxy. To forget that essential fact is to annul all the rest.

4. **Sins of the tongue and sins of wealth are just as grave today as James indicated they were in his own day.**

This cannot be stressed too many times. We live in an age where the gulf between rich and poor, even among Christians, is impossible to ignore. Worse than that, there are Christians who stridently promote laissez-faire capitalism or promote a "gospel of wealth," despite the fact that they have no authentic support for such ideas in the teachings of the New Testament.

Those who are rich have an obligation to share their wealth. There is no getting around the clear and repeated message of the Scriptures on this matter without belying the faith they proclaim. Likewise, in a period in which "the tongue"—including its extensions like the keyboard—is untamed, coarse, loud, insulting, and vicious (even among Christians), James's exhortations are more relevant than ever. Or, as Jesus said with no mincing of words:

> You brood of vipers, how can you, being wicked, speak of good things? For the mouth speaks out of what overflows from the heart. The good man issues good things out of his good stores, and the wicked man issues wicked things out of his wicked stores. But I tell you that every idle word that men will speak, they will render an account of it on the day of judgment; for by your words you shall be vindicated, and by your words you shall be condemned. (Matt 12:34–37)

The pastoral ministry today, if it is not addressing both the evils of unshared wealth and unrestrained mouths, is failing in its responsibility.

5. **The Christian community is intended to be one of mutual support, mutual confession, mutual prayer, mutual healing, and equality.**

James's model church was the mother church of the faith—the apostolic community in Jerusalem. In Acts 2 and 4, it is presented as the ideal. And it is that same ideal vision of a community of love—the living embodiment of the kingdom Jesus proclaimed (the "salt of the earth," "the light of the world," "a city set upon a hill," the light of which should "shine out before men, so that they may see your good works and may glorify your Father in the heavens"; Matt 5:13–16)—which underlies his exhortations in his letter. The only way that this can be realized among any assembly of disciples is by a firm intention to make it happen, which is to say, by a renewed determination to obey the words of Christ.

Today's world is starving for such a community of love, free of wrangling and strife, free of viciousness and appeals to violence, determined to hold itself and its witness together even when differences strain the fellowship of believers. That should be our renewed vision in a troubled age, and James's epistle reminds us that it is what we should pursue. The "royal law" should guide us in all things, and those with pastoral responsibilities should serve that law first and promote it with zeal. Without a prior adherence to the heft of Christ's "royal law," our theology and doctrinal stances are without weight in the world, waiting merely to be swept away if the wind should blow ill. Without love between Christians, even the creed rings hollow.

And this is why the Letter of James is so important for us today.